Published by Rhonda Wilson-Dikoko
Publishing partner: Paragon Publishing, Rothersthorpe

© Rhonda Wilson-Dikoko 2022

The rights of Rhonda Wilson-Dikoko to be identified as the author of this work have been asserted by her in accordance with the Copyright, Designs and Patents Act of 1988. All rights reserved; no part of this publication may be reproduced, stored in a retrieval system, or transmitted in any form or by any means, electronic, mechanical, photocopying, recording or otherwise without the prior written consent of the publisher or a licence permitting copying in the UK issued by the Copyright Licensing Agency Ltd. www.cla.co.uk

ISBN 978-1-78222-932-2

Book design, layout and production management by Into Print
www.intoprint.net
+44 (0)1604 832149

© Copyright, 1957,
By FRANK CHARLES THOMPSON
Entered at Stationers' Hall, London
Previous Editions
Copyright, 1908, 1917, 1929, 1934
All Rights Reserved Throughout the World

Scripture taken from the New King James Version ®. Copyright ©1982 by Thomas Nelson, Inc. Used by permission. All rights reserved.

The HOLY BIBLE, NEW INTERNATIONAL VERSION ®, NIV ®. Copyright ©1973, 1978, 1984, 2011 by Biblica, Inc. ™ Used by permission of International Bible Society ®. All rights reserved worldwide.

"Scripture taken from THE MESSAGE. Copyright ©1993, 1994, 1995, 1996, 2000, 2001, 2002. used by permission of NavPress Publishing Group."

"Scripture taken from THE AMPLIFIED BIBLE. Old Testament copyright ©1965, 1987 by The Zondervan Corporation. The Amplified New Testament copyright ©1958, 1987 by The Lockman Foundation. Used by permission."

The Holy Bible, Berean Study Bible, BSB Copyright ©2016, 2020 by Bible Hub. Used by Permission. All Rights Reserved Worldwide.

"Scripture is taken from GOD'S WORD ®, ©1995 God's Word to the Nations. Used by permission of Baker Publishing Group."

"Scripture quotations are from The Holy Bible, English Standard Version ®, copyright ©2001 by Crossway, a publishing ministry of Good News Publishers. Used by permission. All rights reserved."

Scripture quotations marked (NLT) are taken from the Holy Bible, New Living Translation, copyright © 1996, 2004, 2007 by Tyndale House Foundation. Used by permission of Tyndale House Publishers, Inc., Carol Stream, IL 60188. All rights reserved. Used by permission.

"Scripture taken from The Voice™. Copyright © 2008 by Ecclesia Bible Society. Used by permission. All rights reserved. Used by permission."

A word from the Editor

Evangelist Rhonda Wilson-Dikoko and I first met when we were both speakers at a ladies' conference, organised by Dr. Adeyemi-Bero in The Hague, Holland; we began to have more contact 6 years ago through my online Devotionals. I purchased her *Release the Dove* books and began to see more of her heart. But it was not until I was editing her newest book, *The Sacred Words of a Sage Femme* that I began to see the extent of this Woman of God's ministry.

You will be blessed and amazed as you read of the inspiring testimonies of changed lives and circumstances through her prayers, insightful teaching, revelation, and loving care – all because of her tenacious faith in our Great God!

Evangelist Rhonda, it has been an honour to help you birth your new baby, *The Sacred Words of a 'Sage Femme'!* Thank you for this privilege! God's peace and blessings to you!

Rev. Helen Jesze, United Kingdom
Author and Speaker, Devotionalsjust4you

Cassandra Scott's Ministry

Leaving Holland, I knew from the many prophecies and words of knowledge that I would be involved in deeper intercessory prayer. It had been prophesied that I would '*minister around my table,*' which I have done most of my 30 years abroad, COVID just made it more frequent and global via zoom.

I had been commissioned as a *Sage Femme* in 1992 and began writing this book in 2017. Returning to the USA, I had the '*What*' I would be doing in ministry, but I did not have the '*Who*' till I met Dr Cassandra Scott, a *Sage Femme* located in Pearland, Texas. Our Ministries run parallel and when we met for the first time, our *babies* leapt like with Mary and Elisabeth. I am eternally grateful that God caused our paths to cross. I have learned so much more about intercession in the short time I've known her. I am so blessed to have Dr Scott endorse my book!

✳✳✳

Rhonda is a woman after God's own heart. She has dedicated her life as a vessel of our Lord and Savior to train and equip men and women all over the world through the gospel and prayer. She lives to point everyone to God.

She embodies the qualities and principles in this written work. Her love, respect, beauty, support and confidence in me and our ministry has helped us understand the gifts and essence of womanhood and a life sold out to our Father.

Our ministries are so much better through our connection to empower intercessors all over the world in our tribe of Issachar 7th Generation.

Cassandra Scott Ministries
Turning Point Faith Ministries
CSM Global Prayer Homes

Dr. Cassandra Scott
Pastor, Author, Mentor
Recipient of Presidential Lifetime Achievement Award, signed by President Joe Biden, presented by Ambassador Jason Renville.

Acknowledgements

To The True Promise Keeper, Way Maker, and Light in the Darkness, I worship you. All your promises to me have been unfolding in my life with few exceptions. I give you glory and honor Almighty God, my Father and Confidant. From the words of the great Apostle Paul, *"For in Him we live and move and have our being. As some of your own poets have said, 'We are his offspring.'"* (Acts 17:2 NIV).

I would like to thank Reverend Helen Jesze for her *assez dur* tenacity in editing this book, spurring me forward to completion.

Much gratitude to my mom, Arlelia Wilson and Aunt Annie (in her heavenly abode) for being the very first *'Sage Femmes'* in my life. Your guidance and advice (second to that of the Holy Spirit) have been humongous in my success in marriage and life in general. Your experiences have not only shaped my character but often been the voice in my head for many decisions taken, as I grew up watching just how wise you both were! I am ever so grateful to you!

To my *LIFE SUPPORT 'SAGE FEMMES'*: Lois Saunders and Sarah Banks, you are my real *'Yokewomen'* who have proven true to their vocation. Your labor and love have not been in vain.

I would like to thank all my Spiritual Children or friends who have gladly shared their God experiences on these pages to be a testament of God's faithfulness and to help somebody on their journey with the Lord.

Thank you, Danielle, for partnering with me all these years to get my work out to the public. Your skills in graphic design and marketing are exceptional.

Words cannot express my deepest gratitude to my husband and best friend, who knows me better than anyone else. After 35 years of marriage, we finish one another's sentences, laugh at each other's jokes, and are dedicated to completing this journey together. Thank you for your life-long support!

Below are three of my personal 'Sage Femmes': My mom, Sis. Sarah during a Missionary Trip to Rwanda where we stopped in Kenya. Here she is with two members of the Masai Tribe. My precious Aunt Annie, my father's sister is on the right.

Table of Contents

Table of Contents

A word from the Editor 4
Cassandra Scott's Ministry 5
Acknowledgements 6
About the Author 8
Foreword 10
Introduction 12
Nicole's Re-story 51
Gary's Re-story 71
David and Jody Jackson's Re-story, USA 74
Faith's Re-Story 78
An Oasis in Malaysia 82
Elena's Re-story 85
Amelie's Re-story 90
Thozama's Re-story 100
Nathalie's Re-story 105
Chelsa's Re-story 108
Kirsten's Re-story 110
Viki's Re-story, ... 112
Daria's Re-story 113
Lupita's Re-story 116
Pastor Lisa Great's Re-story 118
Hazel's Re-story 119
Hannelie's Re-story 121
Esther's Re-story 123
Dorothy's Re-story 128
Poems and Sacred Reflections 136
Epilogue – By Fabien Zinga 159
Postlude 161

About the Author

Rhonda Wilson-Dikoko was born in Fayette, Alabama on February 3, 1964. Her father urged her to study nursing after High School, so she did. But her real passion was journalism. She dabbled in it during High School and later took courses in Creative Writing.

Rhonda married Clement Dikoko from Congo, Africa, in 1986 and moved to Congo in 1988. Rhonda considers herself a Global Citizen. She and her husband, now both ministers, have lived in many different countries, on 4 continents doing ministry wherever they go. They have 3 children Alesea, twins Obialet and Danielle, a son-in- law Carmelo and two grand-children Olivier and Sanaa.

Rhonda's Ministry has spanned over 30 years with an emphasis on Women's Ministry and under-privileged children. Rhonda hails from Double Portion Church where she was ordained in 2001 under the auspices of Pastor Hayse Moss and the late Evangelist Sarah Banks. Rhonda is fluent in French and traveled for many years with Sis. Sarah (as many fondly call her) as her personal interpreter.

Rhonda was the Bible Study Leader for Oasis in Malaysia for 6 years. She loves to empower women and help stir up their passion for Jesus as well as discover their giftings. Her vision was for Oasis members from their various walks of life to start up Oasis Satellites wherever they go. That is already coming into fruition.

Rhonda was Director of an Orphanage in Pointe Noire and helped to fund-raise for that orphanage, and for many other outreaches and causes she might have stumbled upon during her travels.

She and her husband currently reside in Texas, USA. Rhonda teaches Bible Study online and is involved in CSM (Cassandra Scott's Ministry) Prayer Ministry. She and her husband are members of The Woodlands Church where they are volunteers on the Welcome and Medical Teams.

Above, Rhonda in her kitchen in Texas where she and her husband love to entertain, feeding people spiritually, emotionally, and physically. There is always room around her table – a circle of love! Below, Clement and Rhonda with youngest children: Obialet and Danielle, Christmas 2021. And Rhonda and Clement a few years ago in their haven, in Georgia.

Foreword

"The older women, likewise, that they be reverent in behavior, not slanderers, not given to much wine, teachers of good things – that they admonish the young women to love their husbands, to love their children, to be discreet, chaste, homemakers, good, obedient to their own husbands, that the word of God may not be blasphemed." (Titus 2:3,4,5 NKJV).

This jewel of a book, **'Sacred Words of a 'Sage Femme'** (midwife) is written from a place of love and deep relationships with those Rhonda has mentored, as a mother in the Faith. A spiritual mentor or midwife if you will, is one that guides you not only in words of wisdom, but in assisting you in fasting and prayer, providing Scriptures, literally assisting you, 'on the stool of life' as you give birth to your project, life, marriage, children or whatever it might be that you are walking through or giving birth to, at any season of life.

You will find these stories from women around the globe to be very touching and inspiring. Ms. Rhonda is one of the most driven and Holy Spirit filled women that I have ever met. There seems to be no end to her compassion and mercy for anyone who is hurting or in need. I was one of those women.

I first met Ms. Rhonda in 2013 Kuala Lumpur, Malaysia. Ms. Rhonda came into my life like a whirlwind, full of faith, joy, and a surety in God that I had never seen before. She daily walks out what she believes, not just in front of others, but wherever she is. I had never heard of a spiritual mentor when I met her. I was in dire need of direction and deliverance. Ms. Rhonda is a hands-on woman of God that will not stop knocking on the doors of Heaven until she gets an answer, she fights the enemy on her knees for her spiritual sons and daughters.

"Preach the word! Be ready in season and out of season. Convince, rebuke, exhort, with all longsuffering and teaching." (2 Tim. 4:2 NKJV).

Rhonda's stories of the **'Sage Femme'** will make you laugh, cry, and cause you to rejoice in the victories of many. So, grab your favorite warm beverage, a cozy blanket and curl up on your favorite chair, sit back and be encouraged and challenged to become a 'Sage Femme' to someone in need.

I was in need, and Ms. Rhonda was my **'Sage Femme.'** I am a new woman because of Ms. Rhonda's 'Yes' to serve the hurting and needy of this world for Jesus.

Carol Smart
Servant of God
Wife, Mother & Grandmother
Friend

Carol in Arizona. Right: In Malaysia at an Oasis Meeting.

Behold! The manifestation of the sons and daughters of Almighty God!

¹⁸ "I consider that our present sufferings are not worth comparing with the glory that will be revealed in us. ¹⁹ For the creation waits in eager expectation for the children of God to be revealed. ²⁰ For the creation was subjected to frustration, not by its own choice, but by the will of the one who subjected it, in hope ²¹ that the creation itself will be liberated from its bondage to decay and brought into the freedom and glory of the children of God. ²²We know that the whole creation has been groaning as in the pains of childbirth right up to the present time. ²³ Not only so, but we ourselves, who have the first fruits of the Spirit, groan inwardly as we wait eagerly for our adoption to sonship, the redemption of our bodies. ²⁴ For in this hope we were saved. But hope that is seen is no hope at all. Who hopes for what they already have? ²⁵But if we hope for what we do not yet have, we wait for it patiently." **(Romans 8:18-25 NIV)**

Introduction

I began writing this book in 2017 in gorgeous destinations such as Paris, St Cloud, and the French Alps.

The Bible declares (in Romans 8:19-21 from the Berean Bible):

"Consider that our present sufferings are not comparable to the glory that will be revealed in us. [19]The creation waits in eager expectation for the revelation of the sons of God. [20]For the creation was subjected to futility, not by its own will, but because of the One who subjected it, in hope [21]that the creation itself will be liberated from its bondage to decay and brought into the freedom and glory of the children of God."

The Lord is waiting for his sons and daughters to be revealed. He has created us with purpose. *"We are saved by grace and that is not of ourselves but a gift from God."* (Ephesians 2:8 NIV). But there are also works created for us in advance. These works are lying dormant waiting for the sons and daughters to manifest, rise and accomplish their purpose. These works are created for your purpose and for you to fulfill. These works do not save you but have been designed, assigned, and designated for you to accomplish.

'Sage Femme' Midwives' Tales

One of my best friends Tina Meijssen, who is from Oman in the Middle East, is a *'Sage Femme'* by profession, in English meaning 'midwife'. This morning, I sat at her kitchen table in her summer home in France lingering over coffee, scrumptious figs and dates and chatting with her friend, Natalie, who was also visiting and a midwife by profession. It was a joy to share with both midwives the title of my book and to let them know that I had used a few of our precious moments together to add to this unscripted devotional.

Ironically the evening before, I had barely slept due to my friend Carol's daughter-in-law being in labor (I fondly refer to Carol as my *'Gem Friend'* because she simply is more precious than a Gem to me). The prayer request was to pray due to an accelerated heartbeat and to pray specifically, because the doctors thought the baby was breech. The wonderful midwives gave me much wisdom about their experience in birthing babies. I was amazed to hear that only with the span of their hand they could make accurate calculations on when and how the baby would be born. They could measure the fetal heart rate and determine the baby's weight only by looking at the mother's tummy! They reassured me that Carol's daughter-in-law would be fine, and she was.

God has given me a role as a Spiritual *'Sage Femme'* to birth spiritual children into this world through prayer and wise counsel as well as through years of experience. I've learned to measure their spiritual growth through their progress in life.

The Book of Isaiah, Chapter 49, has been my guide as I have endeavored to administer wise counsel and encouragement to so many, through the leading and guidance of the Holy Spirit. I have tried to clothe myself in wisdom through these precious verses of scripture:

When Solomon wisely asked God for discernment to lead the Great People of God, this was Father's response. *"12 I will do what you have asked. I will give you a wise and discerning heart, so that there will never have been anyone like you, nor will there ever be. 13 Moreover, I will give you what you have not asked for—both wealth and honor—so that in your lifetime you will have no equal among kings. 14 And if you walk in obedience to me and keep my decrees and commands as David your father did, I will give you a long life."*

This is a Sacred Promise that I claim. Notice that someone like Solomon who was born from an adulterous woman could have such favor with God! This is proof to all of us that "**Your past does not disqualify you for claiming and receiving the blessings of the Lord in your life!**"

Being a Virtuous Woman

Many women seem to think that Proverb 31 NIV is unattainable. They think that it takes many women to accomplish those tasks and not just one. I disagree. I have claimed this scripture for myself and those who know me *well* can attest that I have fulfilled most or at least come close to attaining all of them. I challenge you to do the same. Scripture says in Proverbs 31:26 NIV, *"She speaks with wisdom, and faithful instruction is on her tongue."* That is a Dunamis scripture to behold and one that is completely attainable.

Proverbs 31 NIV is my "Mantra" and daily Challenge to become a wife of Noble Character.

Proverbs 31: 10-31 NLV – A Wife of Noble Character

10 Who can find a virtuous and capable wife?
   She is more precious than rubies.
11 Her husband can trust her,
   and she will greatly enrich his life.
12 She brings him good, not harm,
   all the days of her life.
13 She finds wool and flax
   and busily spins it.
14 She is like a merchant's ship,
   bringing her food from afar.

*¹⁵ She gets up before dawn to prepare breakfast for her household
   and plan the day's work for her servant girls.
¹⁶ She goes to inspect a field and buys it;
   with her earnings she plants a vineyard.
¹⁷ She is energetic and strong,
   a hard worker.
¹⁸ She makes sure her dealings are profitable;
   her lamp burns late into the night.
¹⁹ Her hands are busy spinning thread,
   her fingers twisting fiber.
²⁰ She extends a helping hand to the poor
   and opens her arms to the needy.
²¹ She has no fear of winter for her household,
   for everyone has warm[c] clothes.
²² She makes her own bedspreads.
   She dresses in fine linen and purple gowns.
²³ Her husband is well known at the city gates,
   where he sits with the other civic leaders.
²⁴ She makes belted linen garments
   and sashes to sell to the merchants.
²⁵ She is clothed with strength and dignity,
   and she laughs without fear of the future.
²⁶ When she speaks, her words are wise,
   and she gives instructions with kindness.
²⁷ She carefully watches everything in her household
   and suffers nothing from laziness.
²⁸ Her children stand and bless her.
   Her husband praises her:
²⁹ "There are many virtuous and capable women in the world,
   but you surpass them all!"
³⁰ Charm is deceptive, and beauty does not last;
   but a woman who fears the Lord will be greatly praised.
³¹ Reward her for all she has done.
   Let her deeds publicly declare her praise.*

The qualities spelled out in these verses appear to be unattainable for today's modern woman. Either she does not aspire to do all these things, or the ability and time alludes her. I like to encourage every woman that I mentor to ascribe to becoming a virtuous woman. There is a famous saying,
'Behind every good man is a good woman,' and I vouch that this indeed is an honorable expression and has proven true on multiple occasions in my experiences.

Proverbs 14:1 NIV says, *"The wise woman builds her house, but the foolish tears it down with her own hands."* It is a well-known fact that if you come to me with a marital issue, even before discussing with your husband, I will ask you to do some self-reflection and look at areas that you can change to better yourself. Often, I have found that when I make a sincere effort to change, then I see a change in my husband as well. Self-improvement improves your marriage and your home.

Always think of the bigger picture: to leave an inheritance of non-divorce for your children. The few whom I have walked on the path of divorce have mostly regretted their decision and remain in contact with their ex-spouse, the children have suffered greatly and have grown up in a broken home. That is only what my experience has been outside of the USA. Divorce should be looked at case by case as there are certainly couples who married wrong partners to begin with or who were non-believers and go on to find happiness elsewhere. I'm most certainly no authority on that topic and nor do I aspire to be. The Bible is our best reference point. Nevertheless, I like to be that Sage Femme who gets in the middle of your mess with you and walk through the mirage of mistrust, lies, fragmented dreams and try to help you salvage some of that.

God is writing a new chapter in your life and can make something beautiful out of those broken pieces, a true re-story. (One of my beautiful Bible study hostesses coined the phrase, '*God is doing a re-story*' and I snatched it up for the context of many of the stories you will read in this book).

God says in Malachi 2:16 that He hates divorce. In Hebrews 13:4b MSG the Bible reads, "*Honor marriage and guard the sacredness of sexual intimacy between wife and husband. God draws a firm line against casual and illicit sex.*" Marriage is hard and it seems much easier to just walk away from the hardship. That's why I like to get in real close with the couple and help them navigate the stormy waters.

There is only once or twice in my entire ministry that I have thought separation or divorce was the only recourse for a couple. Please note this was after months and even years of walking with one couple, counseling and even bringing the woman into my home for protection when she was in grave danger.
When I arrive at that point of thought, I still allow the woman or man to make that decision on their own through careful prayer and meditation with the Father. In one of these cases the woman was in acute danger and the Lord provided a way out for her and her children to escape to another country! The Lord went ahead of them and provided schools in that country and accommodations.

The other case was similar as the young woman was also thrown out of her home! I brought her to live with me for a time until she was stable. My husband and I provided a safe place for her husband to come for mediation, but the marriage still ended in divorce. They had been unequally yoked from the beginning.

I sincerely believe when a woman or man are in a life and death situation in their home, the Lord will provide a safe passage to a haven, then walk you through the next steps of what you should do. I've seen it time and time again.

For this reason, I implore young women to rather aspire to be what the passage in Proverbs 31 describes. Perhaps it may save your home in due course or at least you would have done all to sustain your castle. A virtuous woman is a 'Jewel' who is both trustworthy and an entrepreneur. She is hard working, raises her children well and speaks highly of her husband. He is well respected.

I prophesy to every woman or man reading this book, *"Your wife shall be like a fruitful vine within the innermost part of your house; Your children will be like olive plants around your table,"* (Psalm 128:3 AMP). *"Your men shall all be men of valor, like David esteeming the Lord always, asking forgiveness when you fall."*

One of the most misconstrued and misunderstood passages in the Bible is from Ephesians 5:21-32 NIV which says, *[21] "Submit to one another out of reverence for Christ. [22] Wives, submit yourselves to your own husbands as you do to the Lord. [23] For the husband is the head of the wife as Christ is the head of the church, his body, of which he is the Savior. [24] Now as the church submits to Christ, so also wives should submit to their husbands in everything.*
[25] Husbands, love your wives, just as Christ loved the church and gave himself up for her [26] to make her holy, cleansing her by the washing with water through the word, [27] and to present her to himself as a radiant church, without stain or wrinkle or any other blemish, but holy and blameless. [28] In this same way, husbands ought to love their wives as their own bodies. He who loves his wife loves himself. [29] After all, no one ever hated their own body, but they feed and care for their body, just as Christ does the church— [30] for we are members of his body. 31 "For this reason a man will leave his father and mother and be united to his wife, and the two will become one flesh." [32] This is a profound mystery—but I am talking about Christ and the Church."

As a child, I used to love reading mystery books. I devoured Nancy Drew books and watched Scooby Doo mystery cartoons on Saturdays. Paul uses the term *mystery*, a common word in this letter (Ephesians 1:9; 3:3, 4, 6, 9; 6:19). The *mystery* he has in mind here is not marriage, but the relationship between 'Christ and the church.' It was not revealed—explained—prior to the time of Christ, but it was now clear Jesus had come to offer salvation to all people, making one family of both Jews and Gentiles who believe in Jesus as Savior.

In the context of marriage, this idea also applies. Paul has just described how a wife ought to submit to their husbands as to Christ, and husbands ought to love their wives as Christ loved the church. Here, he connects these threads into the idea that all believers, regardless of race or gender, are equally heirs of God through Jesus Christ.

Paul further explains how Christian husbands and wives should apply their understanding of salvation within their marriage. Wives are commanded to *'submit'* to their husbands as they would to Christ, and to show them respect. Often overlooked, however, is that men are equally obligated. Husbands are told to love their wives as Christ loved the church: with humility and sacrifice, as if caring for their own bodies. Despite popular myth, the Bible does not permit either sex to be abusive or unloving within a marriage.

If you want to see God's perfect plan and design for man and woman, go back and read Genesis before The Fall. Everything was perfection and worked in harmony. The man and the woman were partners and in good standing relationship with God. There was transparency and nothing was hidden until the ANCIENT serpent came on the scene.

The man was given complete dominion to rule the earth and name the animals. The woman was created as his *azer*, which means a helper like unto God.

In Genesis 2:18 NIV, when God provided a helper for Adam, He used a glorious Hebrew word for helper: *azer (A-ZER)*.

Then the Lord God said, "It is not a beneficial thing for the man to be alone. I will make for him an azer who is his complement or equal." ^{21} *So the Lord God caused the man to fall into a deep sleep; and while he was sleeping, he took one of the man's ribs and then closed up the place with flesh.* ^{22} *Then the Lord God made a woman from the rib he had taken out of the man, and he brought her to the man.* ^{23} *The man said, "This is now bone of my bones and flesh of my flesh; she shall be called 'woman', for she was taken out of man."*

In Hebrews, *azer* is used 19 times; mostly it is used to denote humanity's great helper. In a world where divorce rates have descended but are still high, it is of utmost importance for a man **to find a 'helper like unto GOD', wouldn't you think?**

The word means a **'helper like unto God.'** God paid a compliment to women with this word. The same word is used in Psalm, where it says, *"O Israel, trust in the Lord, for He is their **'Helper and shield'.**"* (Psalm 115:9 NIV).

The term is always used to describe someone who brings significant help. When the ancient Hebrew speaking Adam heard the term used to describe Eve, he would have been impressed. He would have thought of women, therefore, as a God-like gift from God. Ephesians 5 is a beautiful chapter for Christian households. It speaks of the mystery of marriage, Christ, and the Church. Considering what we have just spoken of as the wife being a helper, an azer if you will for HER husband, I want to speak briefly on the topic of *'Surrendering.'* Ephesians 5:21 NIV, ^{21} *"Submit to one another out of reverence for Christ."*

For the sake of understanding 'submit' better, let's interchange it with 'to *surrender.'* You revere and love the Lord and you know He loves you back thus you are willing to submit or surrender yourself to Him. You've heard of the song, *I Surrender All*.

All to Jesus I surrender,
All to Him I freely give;
I will ever love and trust Him,
In His presence daily live.

> *I surrender all,*
> *I surrender all.*
> *All to Thee, my blessed Savior,*
> *I surrender all.*

All to Jesus I surrender,
Humbly at His feet I bow,
Worldly pleasures all forsaken;
Take me, Jesus, take me now.

All to Jesus I surrender,
Make me, Savior, wholly Thine;
Let me feel Thy Holy Spirit,
Truly know that Thou art mine.

All to Jesus I surrender,
Lord, I give myself to Thee;
Fill me with Thy love and power,
Let Thy blessing fall on me.

All to Jesus I surrender,
Now I feel the sacred flame.
Oh, the joy of full salvation!
Glory, glory to His name!

When I perform a wedding, I love reading God's intention of marriage which says: *"The union of husband and wife is intended by God for their mutual joy; for the help and comfort given each other in prosperity and adversity; and, when it is God's will, for the procreation of children and their nurture in the knowledge and love of the Lord. Therefore, marriage is not to be entered into unadvisedly or lightly, but reverently, deliberately, and in accordance with the purposes for which it was instituted by God."*

Now Proverbs 18:22 says, *"He who finds a wife finds a good thing and obtains favor from the Lord."*

Therefore, a man who finds a wife has found someone who will be good and beneficial for his well-being and life in general while he remains on planet earth. MEN! YOU'VE FOUND A GOOD THING AND you are highly favored by God! Wives, you have now become an azer, a helper like unto God for your man. When marriage is played out as God has intended, both parties are exuberant although there will be struggles, trials and tribulations (1 Corinthians 7:28 NIV), when you keep to God's design and place Him in the center, marriage works so much better!

An azer as stated earlier, is a helper like unto God. In the garden of Eden, there was pure harmony. I long to have lived during that time. But I'm reminded by Holy Spirit that Eden will be restored. However, we will not have a second chance at marriage as we know it here on the earth. The only marriage in Eternity will be with Christ, the Groom and His Bride, The Universal Church, the *Iglesias*. Our only opportunity is to get our marriage right is here on earth. This creates in me a deep desire not to give up on this Sacred Covenant God has granted us to enjoy life together.

Ecclesiastes 4:12b "A cord of three strands is not easily broken." This means you must keep Jesus in the center of your marriage. My 'Mom Project' when Mom stayed with me for six months in 2021 was to make lovingly hand stitched pillows. When you braid two ROPEs together, they can possibly break but three strands are not easily broken. The knots are closely together and tight, that's how your marriage should be! God, the husband, and the wife make up the three strands that are not easily broken!

Pastor Lisa and I (you'll read her re-story later in this book) began our first women conferences in Malaysia after I read a book by Laura Doyle on "The Surrendered Wife." This book had been recommended to me by my Pastor and mentor, Sarah Banks. She had spent much time with me in my home as well as traveling on ministry trips and I thought perhaps she had seen that something was awry in my relationship towards my husband. Therefore, I dutifully procured a copy of the book and proceeded to read it but had to put it down multiple times as the concepts and principles in that book were foreign to my DNA and my body, mind and soul rejected the concepts!

Fortunately, I trusted my midwife and mentor, Sis Sarah and finally was able to complete the book and begin to practice the principles during one of my vacations while home in the USA. I remember being particularly frustrated with my husband for lack of making the 'right decisions' on where to stay on vacation, what type of vehicle to rent, which restaurants to go to, so this time, I decided to let it ALL go and to let Clement handle it with little input from me. I was pleasantly surprised that by the end of the summer, there had been fewer arguments and we had experienced a fun filled vacation! I had been pampered by my husband who had decided to rent an SUV due to a prior injury I had sustained (I would never have paid for that upgrade)! He also made excellent choices on upscale hotels to stay and restaurants to dine! His driving, which I had badgered him on in the past, was less aggravating to me as I simply prayed and allowed Holy Spirit to take the reins! Did a miracle occur in my life and marriage? It most certainly did, and it began with me changing me and allowing God in 'my mundane!'

The Set-Up

I met my husband on the University of Alabama campus in 1987. It was not a whirl-wind romance that I had so desired, being the hopeless romantic that I am. But it was a relationship that developed over time through a friendship.

My girlfriend and I were going to a laundry-mat to wash clothes. We were dressed down, not at all attractive. However, Toni was one of those model-perfect, beautiful dark-skinned girls that even without makeup, her beauty brought attention to her. This was the situation on that faithful Sunday morning.

Clement (now my husband) was showing Amadu around campus when Toni caught Amadu's eye. He could not speak English so had Clement translate for him. They invited us to their apartment for beer and pizza. I was reluctant as I was living a life of celibacy having survived a toxic relationship, my goal was to focus on my education. I had not dated or had a relationship in a long while and did not want any of that to change, therefore my answer was an emphatic '*No*'. Toni pleaded with me to accompany her just for a while since she could not understand their accents! So, I succumbed. Only staying long enough to have pizza and beer, I exited, leaving Toni there to commence a relationship with these African men who were students at the UA (University of Alabama). This was the genesis of me becoming acquainted with Clement and later a relationship developed.

When Clement proposed, I was reluctant to accept. I had my doubts on so many levels, but my mother and aunt were very persuasive in their arguments. Surprisingly, they felt we were a match from Heaven, and he would have a good influence on me.

We wed on December 6, at Double Portion Church in Northport, Alabama. That day held a series of events that caused me to doubt our decision. A client where I worked had previously invited me to what had now become my home church, Double Portion, where she had been attending. It was there that I was totally delivered and baptized both in water and the Holy Spirit. She discipled me through my early days of being '*born again*'.

This same Christian elder sister in the Lord who had initially shown kindness towards me turned out to be a wolf in sheep's clothing. It appears she had a hidden agenda. She was totally against our marriage. She had hand-picked and chosen a Christian man whom she believed would be right for me. Both this young man and I had been assisting her financially. She had requested that I take out a loan for her in my name which she later defaulted on. I ended up having to pay off her debt to clear my name.

Nevertheless, being the young impressionable new 22-year-old Christian that I was and having been brought up to respect my elders, I did not want to go against her wishes.

She had already become very controlling over my life in terms of my friendships and college roommate. I was caught in the middle and found it hard to navigate the waters concerning her. But in matters of the heart, I knew well enough with my history of failed relationships, that I needed to hear from Father myself on this. So, I treated this elderly Christian friend with kindness, invited her to the wedding and did not follow her advice.

She became angry with me and pronounced all manner of curses over me and to add insult to injury, she did not attend our wedding. Neither did the young man who was a dear friend of mine, whom she wanted me to wed. Later she insulted the pastor of our church, cursed him as well and stopped attending. She caused a lot of confusion.

As for the young man she wanted to hook me up with, he married one month after I did to the sister of an ex-girlfriend, whom he hardly knew. Both my husband and I attended their wedding. In the following year he and his wife were involved in a fatal accident that took both of their lives. I was completely heart-broken for the loss of this dear friend as well as how the tables had turned with this *elder Christian* friend. I am so grateful that I had enough faith in God that this situation did not destroy me but made me stronger.

Treasury of Scripture – Words of Wisdom

Matthew 7:15-16 NIV

15 "Watch out for false prophets. They come to you in sheep's clothing, but inwardly they are ferocious wolve. 16By their fruit you will recognize them. Do people pick grapes from thornbushes, or figs from thistles?"

Also, the Word says in Jeremiah 23:16 ESV:

"This is what the LORD of Hosts says: 'Do not listen to the words of the prophets who prophesy to you. They are filling you with false hopes. They speak visions from their own minds, not from the mouth of the LORD.'"

Beloved, this is very important to know. I have learned through this situation and many others in my life that not only can people be misleading, but dreams and visions may also mislead you. You must exercise discernment. The enemy knows what your desires are. He is clearly capable of conjuring up seemingly true things in your mind, whereby you are duped, completely fooled. Indeed, your own mind can desire something so much that you, too, begin to see the writing on the wall or search for prophecy that will justify your selfish desires.

It is imperative that you take these desires and place them upon the altar of God. You MUST have knowledgeable and wise counselors around you who will tell you the truth, who will pray for you and assist you in understanding God's will for your life.

I once had a dear friend who had been divorced for years but refused to budge in her belief that her husband would return. She died with this desire still in her heart. She chased after prophecies, Words of Knowledge and Scriptures that would justify her desires. No actions on the ex-husband's part justified this belief and besides, she was miserable living where she did, all because she was waiting for her husband to return. Did she truly hear from God?

She was a godly woman, full of the Gifts of the Spirit. I have always tried to assist her in utilizing her gifts more for the Body of Christ. She ran her race with perseverance, and I will always love and respect her for that!

Understand this: your friends love you and want you to be happy. They will usually pray with you for your hopes and desires to come to pass. The first thing you must ask yourself in prayer is what Jesus Himself did, *"Father, if you are willing, take this cup from me; yet not my will, but yours be done"* (Luke 22:42).

Jesus always sought to do the WILL of the Father for His life even if it was painful. Always surround yourself with good advisers who will not just tell you what you want to hear but will tell you the truth.

"Plans fail for lack of counsel, but with many advisers they succeed." Proverbs 15:22 NIV.

The Promise

My brother had recently gotten his driver's license and agreed to accompany our mom and aunt to the wedding. An unfortunate accident occurred while driving in the larger metropolitan city of Tuscaloosa, Alabama. Therefore, my mother and my aunt were not in attendance during our nuptials. Instead, they were in the Emergency Room at the hospital. Fortunately, they had only sustained minor injuries.

December 6, 1986, Double Portion Church, our Wedding

At the end of the wedding as we were ushered out of the hall and into our car, something spectacular took place in the heavenlies that I was only to see a few years later.

There appeared a Promise that the Father had given to all of humanity but on December 6th, that Promise was given specifically to us.

In the sky, there was a rainbow and a light that shone from Heaven upon us. Seven years later, when our marriage was on shaky grounds, the Lord had instructed me to take out that photo, which had been taken by my sister Sarah, who was full of the Holy Spirit. Father instructed me to enlarge the photo and write our wedding Covenant that he had given to me on our wedding day, only for me to discover this seven years later. This is what I was told to write:

"And God said: This is the sign of the covenant I am making between me, you and Clement, a covenant for all generations to come: I have set my rainbow in the clouds, and it will be the sign of the covenant between me, you and Clement. Whenever I bring clouds over the earth and the rainbow appears in the clouds, I will remember my covenant between me, you and your husband and your posterity. Never again will perfidiousness or a breach of trust become a flood to destroy your marriage. Whenever the rainbow appears in the clouds, I will see it and remember the everlasting covenant between God, you and your spouse and all your posterity."

So, God said to Rhonda, *'This is the sign of the covenant I have established between me, you and Clement and all your posterity."*

Looks strikingly familiar, eh? It should. It was taken from the Covenant God gave to Noah in Genesis 9. Now God had put that rainbow in the sky over us to foretell our future. The Lord knew, without it, I would have most likely gone through with my plans to leave on that seventh year. Instead, our God in His infinite mercies carved out a plan that would show me His loving kindness toward us and HIS faithfulness towards our unity.

This Promise is illuminated in the light of the unfortunate occurrence of our wedding photographs. The film was faulty, none of the photos developed! Yes, you have understood correctly. Our professional photographs were all a flop! We have no memories of that beautiful, glorious day, save a few scattered photographs that family and friends had taken.
Looking back, I would rather have this wonderful photo of promise from the Lord God my Father than ALL the photos a professional photographer could deliver. For this single photo held the compass for our lives, the roadmap, the surety, and firm promise from the Lord God Himself.

A Covenant from God is vastly different from a contract from a human being. I speak about this in detail in the Release the Dove Workbook.

Scripture reads in Hebrew 6:13 NIV, *"When God made his promise to Abraham, since there was no one greater for him to swear by, he swore by himself, saying, 'I will surely bless you and give you many descendants'."*

We know the story of Abraham, his faith-walk and his promise of a son being fulfilled through a menopausal Sarah and himself over a hundred years old.

> **God does the impossible. Not only does He perform the impossible, but He does the contrary to what one would think. Just the idea of Mary being impregnated by the Holy Spirit puts medical science in dire straits. One thing l love about God is that He operates in the extraordinary, the miraculous! Those things that are unimaginable.**

Isaiah 55:8-9 NIV declares:

⁸ "'For my thoughts are not your thoughts,
  neither are your ways my ways,'
declares the Lord.
⁹ 'As the heavens are higher than the earth,
  so are my ways higher than your ways
  and my thoughts than your thoughts.'"

HIS WAYS ARE HIGHER.

Dearly Beloved, if you are struggling with a promise that has yet to be fulfilled, I want to encourage you to trust in the Sovereignty of God.
Trust Him with your very life. He made you, wired you, knows what is inside of you. He simply knows best for you.

The Lord God reminded me of His promise in 1992 to bring sons and daughters from every corner of the earth. At the time, I could not fathom the meaning of that Scripture. I came to understand the Sovereignty of our God. What He has purposed, He will accomplish. This was His Promise from Isaiah 49: 8-9, 18-23 NIV.

⁸ "This is what the Lord says:
'In the time of my favor I will answer you,
  and in the day of salvation I will help you;
I will keep you and will make you
  to be a covenant for the people,
to restore the land
  and to reassign its desolate inheritances,
⁹ to say to the captives, Come out,
  and to those in darkness, Be free!

¹⁸ Lift up your eyes and look around;
  all your children gather and come to you.

As surely as I live,' declares the Lord,
  'you will wear them all as ornaments;
  you will put them on, like a bride.'

²² *This is what the Sovereign Lord says:*
'See, I will beckon to the nations,
  I will lift up my banner to the peoples;
they will bring your sons in their arms
  and carry your daughters on their hips.
²³ *Kings will be your foster fathers,*
  and their queens your nursing mothers.
They will bow down before you with their faces to the ground;
  they will lick the dust at your feet.
Then you will know that I am the Lord;
  those who hope in me will not be disappointed.'"

One thing of certainty that I can tell you as a *'Sage Femme'* is, that God's Word NEVER ever falls to the ground. What He promises, He will bring to pass. For us as mere humans, our minds cannot comprehend the workings of God. Because He sees our end from our beginning, my encouragement to you is simply to have faith and to walk with God.

If someone would have told me back then, how my life would have turned out today, I would have said, *'Impossible'*! Yet since God promised those things to me, like Mary, I hid them away deep in my heart and trusted God to bring them to fruition in His own way and most importantly, His own timing. What the scriptures in Isaiah 49 foretell is exactly what happened in my life.

God's timing is impeccable. Not a day later than 430 years did he bring the Israelites out of their captivity in Egypt! Did their previous cries fall on deaf ears? NO! Yet, God had predestined the RIGHT time for their EXODUS, and He has done the same for you! Do not miss the journey! Do not miss the moment! Do not miss the lessons of God's faithfulness in your life!

I find it difficult to develop those verses from Isaiah 49, therefore, instead what I will do, is to allow you to hear from the Spiritual Children God has given me, just as He promised. He has brought them from many nations and diverse backgrounds and tongues, JUST AS HE PROMISED. I stand in awe!

As a midwife, I have been privileged to help these spiritual children or friends birth their brilliance, birth their destinies, and partake of the joy of believing in what God has spoken and seeing it come to pass. This book is a compilation of their stories and God's faithfulness. But first, my story unfolds...

Two years after getting married, I moved to Brazzaville, Congo, Africa. This transition was born through prayer and revelation of my future through God's Word.

Clement got a telex from the University of Marian Ngouabi where he had attended in Brazzaville, urging him to return to Congo for a position as Professor in the Department of Business and Finance. My husband did not hesitate to book his flight for his return. I was devastated. Not once had we discussed that our marriage would involve me leaving my natal country and returning to Congo, Africa with him!

Even at the young and tender age of 23, I knew that prayer was essential for every decision in my life. Therefore, I planned a fast that would prove God. The Bible says in Proverbs 3:5-6 NIV, *"Trust in the Lord with all your heart and lean not on your own understanding, acknowledge him in all your ways and He shall direct your path."* Again, He says in Proverbs 16:3 NIV, *"Commit to the LORD whatever you do, and he will establish your plans."*

I had a wonderful spiritual mom in that city, Sis Lois Saunders whom I never hesitated to call upon for prayer. I started a fast and asked her to agree with me in my proposal to the Lord. I said to God, *"Lord, if it is truly you telling me to move from Alabama to Congo, then allow my husband to call me during this fasting period."* The Scripture I stood upon was, Isaiah 38:7 NIV, *"This is the Lord's sign to you, that the Lord will do what he has promised."*

Now for Millennial readers this might appear as no big deal. But in those days, communication to my husband was faster by mail than by phone!!! Hardly anyone had phones in that country! Especially households. To speak to me, my husband had to go to a cousin who worked for the Telecommunications company, to call me once every couple of months!

In fact, since he had left the USA, I had only spoken to him once or twice, briefly by phone. All our correspondence was via courier! Therefore, my asking God to allow my husband to call me was a big feat and would be a confirmation for me to move to the Congo with my husband. Again, that decision within itself, was enormous.

I was in the process of fulfilling my father's dream for my life. I was working as a nurse at the Veterans Hospital, had received an outstanding evaluation from my Head Nurse and was easing up the echelon ladder of success very quickly. In those days, VA would also pay for one's continued education, so I was planning to return to school.

Therefore, moving to Congo would disrupt my career and education. I needed to be sure I was hearing from God! So, after agreeing with my spiritual mom, Sis. Lois Saunders, I began to pray fervently for an answer from God. To my recollection, the fast was no longer than one or two days at the most. At the end of the second day and before I closed out the day in prayer, my husband called!!!

No other confirmation was required, I wrote my resignation letter to my job at the VA, halted my education, sold my worldly goods and purchased a one-way ticket to Brazzaville, Congo!

Before leaving the USA, my spiritual mom prayed with me once more. In this prayer, she saw a building with columns and described this place perfectly as my next place of employment. In hindsight, her Word of Knowledge assisted me in choosing between working at the World Health Organization or the US Embassy. The place she described was identical to the US Embassy's Building in Congo Brazzaville!

I can never over emphasize the importance of having a Spiritual Mother in your life. God was so gracious to provide one whom I have learned so much from, and love to emulate in my own ministry. Her honesty, faith and relationship with God has helped to shape my spirituality immensely.

Clement and I during my first months in The Congo. I had just turned twenty-four years old. This picture was taken at an American Embassy Official dinner.

Arrival in Congo

I had only flown ONCE in my entire life and that was to visit my husband in Indiana. He had purchased the ticket and spoken to the airline to ensure that I would sit beside a veteran flyer. He insisted that the stewardess assist me in feeling comfortable on my flight! Those were the days before 911 (Collapse of Twin Towers in New York)!!! Then the flying experience was completely different from what it has become today!

I never could imagine that embarking on Sabena Airlines on March 3, 1988, merely one month after my 24th birthday would be a flight of no return.

The flight was like my first one to Indiana, just longer and on a much bigger plane. My fear of flying subsided after boarding and I decided to sit back and enjoy the experience. On that 16-hour flight and approximately 6-hour layover, I couldn't sleep much, due to the excitement and restlessness I had at the prospect of arriving in Congo, Africa for the first time.

When Sabena's flight began its descent over Brazzaville, I was enchanted by the beautiful city lit up with what appeared to be thousands of lights winking at me in earnest and fulfilled promise. There was the famous Congo River separating Congo, Brazzaville from Kinshasa, Zaire.

Clement had purchased a French language book for me, whereby I had learned some rudimentary French such as numbers, salutations, and essential words. I felt like I was equipped to deal with whatever was on the ground.

The airplane continued its descent away from the lights and into a city clothed in darkness. There was a power-cut in Brazzaville and the plane had to be guided by kerosene lighting to make its final descent into Brazzaville, the capital city of Congo. The spectacular Vegas-like lit-up city which I assumed to be Congo had been Kinshasa!

I determined that nothing would squash my excitement of being in this new country. This country girl was up for the challenge. I had not seen my husband in 4 months; therefore, I could barely contain my excitement. My first thing upon exiting the flight was to find a restroom whereby I could freshen up, I didn't do this on the flight. I was in for a rude awakening in this dark airport! The toilets were atrocious, filthy and there was no mirror to see oneself!

Still, I forged ahead knowing that God would not lead me to a wrong destination. I chose to STILL believe; STILL trust and STILL NOT LEAN on my own understanding. These lessons appear simple, but these are ones I deal with daily during my mentoring and counseling sessions.

A Test of my Faith

Armed with the knowledge that Father did not bring me to this city to forsake me, I decided to apply for some jobs earlier on. As a career woman, I wanted to start working right away. I went to the US Embassy, World Health Organization, and a few other places to submit my resume.

The US Embassy *ESPECIALLY* had no openings. There were two French nurses employed and they were not looking to hire anymore. Leaving that building, I stopped to admire the extremely ornate architecture and remembered my spiritual mother's vision. The building was exactly as she had described. Habakkuk 2:2-3 NIV says, *"Write the vision down, it shall surely come to pass."*

My mouth dropped, aghast, thinking of the possibility of being employed by the US Embassy. I left smiling to myself and knowing God was surely up to something!

Meeting the Family

My husband was busy taking me everywhere, introducing me to family and friends. He also wanted us to visit his sister in Pointe Noire, the Oil Capital of Congo. We boarded the Train Blue for this trip. What a remarkable and interesting time we had! I shall NEVER ever forget it as long as I live. The train halts, the food, which was sold, the sounds and sights of Congo – virtually everything was new. It was as if I had gone back a hundred years in time!

When the torrential rains began to flow, an entire expanse of land would seemingly disappear as if it were an avalanche. The already difficult roads with potholes, coupled with standing water, made travel in the city during the rainy season, arduous.

Finally, we arrived in Pointe Noire. I remember for the first time being alone with Clement's sister and being able to express myself in my few French words and to be understood!

Pointe Noire was vastly different from Brazzaville. There was a slower pace. This city was beautiful, surrounded by water. Fish was plentiful and it is here that I learned to eat fish the Congolese way! Not fried but in a soup with vegetables served with plantain or rice. My sister-in-law was an expert chef and housewife. After a week or so, we reluctantly bade them farewell as we headed back to the hustle and bustle of Brazzaville.

When we arrived back home, our neighbors told us of a visit from the US Embassy and a letter for me. They described the government car and tag. They wondered in amazement just who I really was! They were astounded to see a foreign vehicle of that caliber on Poto-Poto soil ('poto-poto' means 'dirt' or 'mud', it is the name of the neighborhood or *quartier* where we lived. It was a very popular *quartier*). You must understand that my husband chose to live in one of the most popular and populous quarters. On one side of the street were the extremely rich, and the other side were the working class and the very poor. This environment did not disrupt my peace and belief in God's Word at all. On the contrary! I would open my wooden windows daily and praise God for a brand-new day!

Our simple home had a bedroom, a freezer, table, and chairs. The bedroom furniture, table and chairs had been a gift from Clement's older brother *Tonton* (big brother) Eugene. The freezer was a gift from *Tantine* (big sister) Louisette. This was my first home in Congo. I was curious about how the neighborhood children would gather around me to peer up at my face, hear me speak or laugh. They would hang around to see whether Tantine would send a command for a Fanta, peanuts, or something else. The children were elated to be sent on errands, not because of what they might get but because it was a society of honor. I remember the delight that would be on their round faces, their bright eyes, I truly relish my time spent in that *quartier*. These first memories are etched not only in my mind but on my heart. There was such a culture of honor. I fit in right away. Most people did not realize that I was even American!

Quickly throwing my bag aside, I ran into the house to open the letter from the American Embassy. Allowing my hands to run over the eloquent lettering, I admired the US seal. My name had been typed out. Slowly, I opened the letter as if it were a precious commodity. It stated that there was a position for me at the Embassy! The second nurse had resigned! God's Word NEVER fails! All His promises are yes and amen to the glory of God!

After only a few short months working as a nurse in the American Embassy, I started feeling excruciating pain in my abdomen. For the diplomats, our embassy utilized an American doctor in the neighboring country of Kinshasa, and she came only once a month. For dire emergencies, we would sometimes use local or French doctors.

By that time, I had lost over 75 lbs. from dieting and sheer arrival in a foreign country, not acclimatizing to the food fare available. The few dishes I could eat consisted of grilled food such as chicken, plantain and sometimes peanuts.
I felt perhaps the pain I was experiencing in my stomach was from peanuts I had eaten at a neighbor's.

As in the welcoming custom of Congo, a casual neighbor had invited me to her home. Her place was not spacious, nor was there any beauty to behold. Yet she held it in such high esteem and cleanliness. She made me feel like such an honored guest. In Congo when you visit someone's home, they always serve juice with peanuts, cookies, or some snacks for their visitors.

When I returned home and slept that night, I awoke with heart wrenching pain in my abdomen like I had NEVER experienced before. My colleague's husband was a French doctor. She arranged a visit to another French doctor who was a colleague of her husband's. Still the pain persisted but subsided after a day or so.

In the meanwhile, my husband was transferred to Pointe Noire, the Oil Capital. He left his job at university to work for an Oil Company in Pointe Noire. His sister and husband dwelt in that place which became a great blessing for me.

Therefore, when the pain recommenced a month or two later after our move, my sister -in-law, Louisette and her husband, Colonel Tabani, took it upon themselves to ensure I benefited from the best health care available in that city. As a Colonel, he had access to the military hospital and made sure I went there. They accompanied me there to be assessed by the military doctors.

This very well might have saved my life as I was admitted to hospital right away. It was discovered that I was pregnant coupled with acute appendicitis. Surgery had to be performed immediately. I only found out about the surgery the night I was being prepped.

Clement and I were so excited about this pregnancy. I already had a name for this beautiful baby whether boy or girl. I had so many visitors from my new job in Pointe Noire as well as one of my dear friends from the US Embassy in Brazzaville. He happened to have been the Deputy of Missions. We used to attend Church with he and his family every Sunday. In fact, he is the one who use to pick us up and together we went to the Protestant Church there.

I was shocked to see the Congolese Military personnel in a frenzy due to his visit. I erred in understanding political protocol and the nature of diplomacy of Government in third world countries. The Military hospital considered my friend's visit as an attempt of a possible coup!

Much later, not only was I astounded to discover the President had sent spies to find out about Clement and myself, but I was fearful. In fact, we had been put on the Government's hit list, unknown to me. Months later, when I heard a click on my home phone, I didn't realize it was the Government listening in. I was often followed and twice, I had been accosted by military soldiers while living in Brazzaville.
It was dangerous for me to be out alone. Colonel Tabani served as a protection for me, and he wanted to ensure my safety while I lived in Pointe Noire.

The following night when I had just drifted off to sleep, the nurses came in to prep me. Though my French was poor, I knew exactly what they were doing, and I had not been informed! I demanded to speak to my husband, but this fell on deaf ears. The prepping continued as I cried and feared for my life. I did not sleep the entire night till Clement came early morning as was his custom. I asked him whether I was to have surgery and he said "No, he wasn't aware," averting his eyes away from me. I could tell he was afraid. I wondered why he would keep this kind of information from me. *"Was something wrong with the baby?"* I thought to myself.

Finally, answers to my fears were confirmed when the doctor came round for his daily visit. He explained that he would have to remove my appendix but would protect the pregnancy during this process. The surgery was imminent; this was the culprit of my pain, according to him. I was not given general anesthetics, just a local epidural. According to the doctor the process to remove the appendix would be expeditious.

The anesthesiologist was kind as she prayed with me, calmed me, and made me feel safe. I clung to Clement before we said our good-byes and they whisked me down the hall into the Operating Room. I was numb from the waist down, otherwise, I was completely aware of my surroundings.

I looked around in this rudimentary operating room. It was basic but clean with only minimal equipment. After scrubbing for surgery, the doctor began the procedure to remove the appendix only to find my pregnancy was ectopic. I had been given only enough anesthesia for the appendix. I literally FELT some of the pain from the latter part of the surgery! The anesthesiologist spoke to me in a soothing hushed tone which enabled me to get through the process miraculously. No additional anesthesia was given.

My left fallopian tube was removed and given to me in a mason jar. I ached for the promise of that baby girl whom I had named *Toleni Genesis*.

The long road ahead involved not only physical but also mental healing. Part of me was numb in the literal sense as well as the spiritual. Today, I now understand this was a sort of depression after the loss of my unborn child. Although I was fortunate just to have survived that operation, I was truly devastated at the loss of my baby and fallopian tube. I questioned the Lord about what He was doing.

On one occasion in 1992 a few years later, the Lord gave me this assurance that I would have physical and spiritual children. The Lord says in Isaiah 55:8-9 NIV, *"'For my thoughts are not your thoughts, neither are your ways my ways' declares the Lord. 'As the heavens are higher than the earth so are my ways higher than your ways and my thoughts your thoughts.'"* We have been exceedingly blessed with three children and two grandchildren who we claim as ours as well!! The Lord has surpassed our expectation, by also blessing me with a host of spiritual sons and daughters who are so very dear to me.

The Lord spoke to me clearly through this passage of Scripture which I have outlined in my ancient Bible, still in my possession today.

Isaiah 49 NIV – *personalized*

"But Rhonda said, 'The Lord has forsaken me,
  the Lord has forgotten me.'
15 Can a mother forget the baby at her breast
  and have no compassion on the child she has borne?
Though she may forget,
  I will not forget you!
16 See, I have engraved you on the palms of my hands;
  your walls are ever before me.
17 Your children hasten back,
  and those who laid you waste depart from you.
18 Lift up your eyes and look around;
  all your children gather and come to you.
As surely as I live,' declares the Lord,
  'you will wear them all as ornaments;
  you will put them on, like a bride.
19 Though you were ruined and made desolate
  and your land laid waste,
now you will be too small for your people,
  and those who devoured you will be far away.
20 The children born during your bereavement
  will yet say in your hearing,
'This place is too small for us;
  give us more space to live in.'
21 Then you will say in your heart,
  'Who bore me these?
I was bereaved and barren;
  I was exiled and rejected.
  Who brought these up?
I was left all alone,
  but these—where have they come from?'
22 This is what the Sovereign Lord says:
'See, I will beckon to the nations,
  I will lift up my banner to the peoples;
they will bring your sons in their arms
  and carry your daughters on their hips.
23 Kings will be your foster fathers,
  and their queens your nursing mothers.
They will bow down before you with their faces to the ground;
  they will lick the dust at your feet.
Then you will know that I am the Lord;
  those who hope in me will not be disappointed.'"

Praying for the Fruit of the Womb

The gift of praying for the Fruit of the Womb, laying hands upon the barren, and getting results that God has given me, has not only been limited to Christians in my sphere of influence but also to non-believers.

The title '*Social Secretary*' was conferred upon me when we resided in Warri, Nigeria. That meant most if not all of the extracurricular fun activities deemed important for expatriates or foreigners were my playground and field of expertise!

On one occasion, after just returning from the USA, I had surprise visitors at my door. "Hello Susan and Philip, how are you both doing?" I said beaming at them and greeting them in the customary French way (by kissing them on both cheeks) and gesturing to them to take a seat in my Livingroom.

"We are doing well, Rhonda," said Susan. "We come bearing good news! We would like for you to organize an African Wedding Reception for us!"

I was elated that a Dutch girl and a French guy would want to have an African wedding in Nigerian Custom! "I would *LOVE* to organize your wedding reception for you. It's going to be a glorious occasion, let's get the entire camp involved!" I laughed, clapping my hands excitedly at the prospect of a party.

We all worked for the same company and lived inside of a gated community manned by armed guards. To go into town, it was mandatory we have armed men accompany us. Therefore, everybody inside the camp relished a distraction of fun activities. As '*Social Secretary*,' I often organized events for the kiddos such as Santa, Easter Bunny, for Valentines I put together a hilarious Newly Weds Game. For Tennis lovers, there would be a Tennis Tournament with lots of fun and games for all, as well as a Fundraiser for a well-known cause.

Therefore, Susan's request was not unusual, she knew I would love the challenge. I looked at her teasingly and said one thing that made her laugh with unbelief! "Susan, everyone I organize weddings for have twins." I took her to my *Baby Wall of Blessings* and showed her all those the Lord had blessed with twins and babies in my ministry. Of course, she laughed even more in disbelief, "You must be joking," she said, looking up at her soon to be husband Philip, who also had a look of sarcasm and utter disbelief on his face but did not dare dampen my spirits.

The wedding reception was an occasion to remember! All nationalities had to wear Nigerian outfits! The event took place at the home of our company Director. We had the *Dowry* for the Bride as well! My husband, Clement, is a fun-loving bloke and in the spirit of fun, fabricated a '*family for the bride and one for the groom.*' There was a *Griot* (Spokesman) for each family per his Congolese custom. Included in the bride's price was a goat, fabrics, whisky, and money!

It was a fabulous time to portray West African culture to the foreigners as well as sponsor an event whereby the entire camp could anticipate...even children attended! Delicious Nigerian food and drink were served in their spirit of hospitality. This successful '*African Wedding Rece*ption' would be an event to remember in the history of the camp.

A few years later we moved to Malaysia, where again some of our Malaysian friends who lived in the camp in Nigeria were back in their native country. We were thrilled to be reunited! One Christmas, Susan, and her husband, for whom we had performed the traditional reception, visited our Malaysian friends for the holidays. We all got together to see them again! I was so touched to see how God had honored my Sacred Words spoken to these Gentile Believers. They presented to me their identical twin girls and this time; I had the last laugh!!!!! Our God IS faithful!

Finding a Good Wife and Family

On another occasion when we were living in Gabon, a young girl from our church in Congo came to visit. Like any other girl her age, she desired to marry and have children. However, she confided in me that her doctor had said she would have problems to conceive. I encouraged her to stay in Gabon and marry a young engineer who was a friend of my husband's. This guy whom I will refer to as Joseph, had accompanied my family and me to the USA the previous year. He had attended a wedding in our church and asked the pastor to pray that he would find a good wife! The Bible declares that he who finds a wife, finds a good thing!

This brilliant and talented engineer was hailed for his accomplishments, having been selected by our company to study in England in one of the top Universities. His photo was placed on the wall of the home office as one of their great scholars. His professional life was sealed, yet he was disappointed not to find a wife of his caliber to enjoy his beautiful life with!

Being the *Matchmaker* that I am, the wheels of my mind started turning. I quickly reminded him of his prayer request at our home church in Alabama. Might this be the *good wife* that he sought after? Having been sorely disappointed in the past with young women, he reluctantly agreed to be introduced to my young protégé from Congo. After meeting her, he protested, complaining that she did not speak the Queen's English and was not the wife he had imagined that he would marry. My young protégé whom I will call, Katrina, also was not enthused saying he simply did not fit the bill of her ideal suitor.

In this dismal environment, I decided to take a back seat to this romance waiting to happen and simply prayed. Katrina was a guest in our home for a few weeks and went with us on several of our outings. I had organized a progressive dinner in which couples commenced at one home for drinks, and instructions on where they would eat their first two courses were given. The starter and entrée would be served in two separate homes and the entire dinner party would meet up in one final home for dessert and coffee. During our aperitif, I noticed there were two singles, Katrina and another friend whose wife was not living in that village. For Gerald and Katrina to participate in the progressive dinner, they would have to be a *'make believe'* couple that evening. I knew this gentleman's wife and felt she wouldn't have a problem with this. The evening was a smashing success and we all ended up back into our respective homes pleasantly full and reminiscing over the events of the evening. We retired for bed so we could be up early for Sunday service.

Sunday's Church was amazing. Looking around in the building, I saw that Joseph was missing. Sunday dinner was at our home today therefore I wondered if he would show up or maybe he was still sulking because of my match-making efforts. I sighed at his play of immaturity.

Back home, I busied myself in the kitchen whilst Katrina helped to set the table. Friends began to arrive but still no sign of Joseph. The day wore on and still no news. I decided to ignore Joseph's blatant absence as he was a constant in our home anyway. When I saw him next, I planned to give him a piece of my mind.

The next day on Monday, Clement and Joseph didn't come for lunch as usual. Now I knew he was purposefully avoiding me. I thought to myself, *"Now this is excessive."* I didn't dare mention my suspicions to Katrina as she was planning to return to the Congo soon.

That evening Clement called me to our bedroom. "Sweetie, I've got to tell you something," he said laughing. "What is it?" I wondered, knowing how he always liked to joke around. "Joseph is upset with us because he thinks we fixed Katrina up with a date over the weekend," he said in hushed tones.

"What?" my mouth flew agape, "He is the one who wasn't interested in her and how dare he accuse me of setting Katrina up with a married man!" I said lowering my voice. Intending to put Joseph in his place, I grabbed my car keys and headed for the door.

"Where are you going so fast?" Clement asked throwing his hands up with an exasperated look on his face.

"Where do you think? To see Joseph of course. Tonight, he will see my true colors!" I said winking my eye in a capricious manner secretly happy that things seemed to be progressing as planned.

As I drove to Joseph's home, I relaxed, rolled my car window down and felt the cool breeze on my cheeks. I smiled to myself. My prayers were truly working and tonight, I would need the grace of God to convince Joseph to see his feelings for what they truly were. The poor soul had been tormented all weekend thinking another man would grab his covenanted Katrina. He was in love and didn't even know it! I had to get him to see it before Katrina left for Congo.

Arriving at Joseph's home, I exited the car and knocked on his front door. He came to the door after a few minutes with a dejected look on his face. He had not eaten in a few days and truly looked gaunt and miserable. "Let's go for a drive," I said to him, "Take your keys, you drive." I said with a backwards glance as I headed to the door.

We sat in silence for a while, driving through the village of Gamba. Sometimes elephants would cross the street, or one could spot a silver-back gorilla slinking into the tropical forest. Once a friend recounted how frightened she had been after spotting a gigantic Boa Constrictor blocking the road after ingesting its prey! She couldn't pass and refused to run over it. That was the only road that led to the city, so she had to either get out of the car and walk over its immoveable body or retreat to the village till the Boa had completed its digestive process and vacated the road. She chose the latter!

Lost in thought, I giggled to myself almost forgetting my assignment.

"Joseph," I said returning to reality, "Why are you doing this to yourself?"

"What?" he asked in a quiet voice.

"You're in love with Katrina, aren't you? Why can't you admit that to yourself?"

At this he pulled to the side of the road and bowed his head. "Is that what it is? I have been so miserable thinking I have lost her. But I have so many conflicting thoughts. She cannot be the one the Lord has sent me, can she? She does not fit any of my criteria."

I spent the next couple of hours counseling with Joseph, helping him to sort out his feelings and to understand faith and fallacy. The ways of God are higher than ours. He had prayed and now God had sent this young woman his way. Would he also refuse her as he had done so many others? Would he miss out on the plans of God for his life and deny his present feelings?

At the end of our conversation, Joseph agreed to try to get to know Katrina better to see whether she was the one. We planned for him to meet her on a few occasions at our home and see how things go. During those times, I made sure to keep the children, myself, and Clement out of the way of their courtship! After a week of this, he invited her to his home.

Later, Katrina recounted in dismay how he had boasted of his expensive wardrobe, his accolades, and his life in general. She looked away in distaste, "*Tantine* Rhonda, I don't think this is the man for me."

I recited to her once more the benefits of marrying someone like him. Besides, their villages were literally next to each other, just from two separate countries! When the French Colonizers divided the land, they hardly took account of the people and families. Instead, they allowed their greed to dictate their property lines resulting in families being separated into another entire country! This was the case of Katrina and Joseph.

"All right, *Tantine*, if you say so. Joseph has invited me to his home again this weekend. Since it's my final weekend here I wasn't sure if I wanted to waste it with him."

Folding my arms, I cocked my head to the side and stared at her with a curious frown on my face but remained silent. Thinking of all the failures this young girl had experienced in her life, the deceptions and now she was given a new opportunity from God but couldn't see it, I shook my head but didn't speak. As a *'Sage Femme'*, sometimes *'Silence'* is the best weapon. Apparently seeing the look on my face, Katrina spoke first.

"Okay, okay, *Tantine*, I'll go one last time and decide if he's the one," she said staring at me as if she'd seen a ghost and quickly retreated to her room. I clapped my hands *'paddy cake'* style (in the *Congolese way*) to exhibit my exasperation while exhaling air from the side of my mouth. This was one of many typical *'nonverbal colloquials'* I'd picked up since living there.

It turned out that last weekend was when Joseph proposed marriage to Katrina after only a few short weeks! We were ecstatic! Clement and I travelled back to the Congo to help organize their traditional wedding. Joseph's job assignment took him to Holland and Katrina followed shortly after. Since then, they have been blessed to live in Holland, Nigeria, USA, Canada and currently they reside in Abu Dhabi.

Fruit of the Womb

My husband and I had the opportunity to visit Joseph and Katrina a few times while they lived in Holland. We were invited with my pastor from the USA to preach in their congregation, so we went. During this time, Katrina spoke in private to my pastor and me about her complications with conception.

We prayed over her and declared she would have a double portion blessing! Shortly thereafter, her twins were born!

As Westerners, you might find this story a bit troubling, figuring I imposed my wishes upon this young couple and interfered in their lives. The truth is, I felt I was being led by the Holy Spirit. This phenomenon of arranged marriage not only occurs in Africa, India, The Middle East, and other nations, but also in the USA.

I wouldn't go so far as to say this was an arranged marriage, forcing this couple to wed, I just saw the potential and helped them along the way. What was implied but I didn't say, is that I knew these two individuals very well and had prayed for both about their lives. I had been a spiritual mom to Katrina during my time in Congo. In Gabon, my husband had taken Joseph as his little brother advising him in his professional and private affairs. But I was the spiritual force in his life. As my mom and auntie had to show me the light, I recognized early that I must do the same for them both. They have been together for over 20 years now. Their twins are at university, and they have a younger son also.

Treasury of Scripture – Words of Wisdom

Consider the story of Abraham and his servant Eleazer

"Abraham was now very old, and the Lord had blessed him in every way. ² He said to the senior servant in his household, the one in charge of all that he had, 'Put your hand under my thigh. ³ I want you to swear by the Lord, the God of heaven and the God of earth, that you will not get a wife for my son from the daughters of the Canaanites, among whom I am living, ⁴ but will go to my country and my own relatives and get a wife for my son Isaac'" (Genesis 24 NIV).

Sarah had passed away, and the complicated role of finding a wife for his precious son fell upon Abraham. Notice, although the servant's name is not given in this passage, most scholars believe his senior servant mentioned in Genesis 15 is the same here. Eleazer's name translates to 'God is help.'

Abraham sent his servant to get a wife for his son Isaac from his own relatives. Before his servant had finished praying, Abraham's great niece Rebekah came out with her jar to draw water from the well. Not only was she from Shem's line, but she was also pure and beautiful. The promised Messiah would come through Abraham's lineage.

¹² "Then he prayed, 'Lord, God of my master Abraham, make me successful today, and show kindness to my master Abraham. ¹³ See, I am standing beside this spring, and the daughters of the townspeople are coming out to draw water. ¹⁴ May it be that when I say to a young woman, 'Please let down your jar that I may have a drink,' and she says, 'Drink, and I'll water your camels too'—let her be the one you have chosen for your servant Isaac. By this I will know that you have shown kindness to my master.'
¹⁵ Before he had finished praying, Rebekah came out with her jar on her shoulder. She was the daughter of Bethuel son of Milkah, who was the wife of Abraham's

brother Nahor. ¹⁶ The woman was very beautiful, a virgin; no man had ever slept with her. She went down to the spring, filled her jar and came up again.
¹⁷ The servant hurried to meet her and said, 'Please give me a little water from your jar.'
¹⁸ 'Drink, my lord,' she said, and quickly lowered the jar to her hands and gave him a drink."

Eleazer could not afford to fail at this fateful task given to him by his Master. Eleazer's journey had been bathed in prayers and notice before he finished praying, he looked up and Rebekah was standing before him! The Word says, *"Before they call, I will answer; while they are yet speaking, I will hear"* (Isaiah 65:24 NIV). He had asked the Lord for specific signs to identify the right woman for Isaac. Scholars say that it must have taken Rebekah 3 hours to water all his camels after they had traveled over 700 miles (perhaps a month) to get to Abraham's relatives. This was indeed no small feat for Rebekah, however this proved to Eleazer she had a servant-like spirit, was hospitable and the one destined for Isaac.

Let's continue the lecture here.

⁵⁷ "Then they said, 'Let's call the young woman and ask her about it.' ⁵⁸ So they called Rebekah and asked her, 'Will you go with this man?'
'I will go,' she said.
⁵⁹ So they sent their sister Rebekah on her way, along with her nurse and Abraham's servant and his men. ⁶⁰ And they blessed Rebekah and said to her,
'Our sister, may you increase
  to thousands upon thousands;
may your offspring possess
  the cities of their enemies.'
⁶¹ Then Rebekah and her attendants got ready and mounted the camels and went back with the man. So, the servant took Rebekah and left."

Both Rebekah's brother, Laban, and her father, Bethuel acknowledged that it was the LORD's will for her to marry Abraham's son.

Since the servant's journey had been successful, he refused to be detained any longer. He wanted to complete the second half of his promise to his master. Having sworn and put his hand under his master's thigh, signified that the promised Messiah would come from Abraham's seed. The servant swore an oath that Isaac's wife would be from Abraham's descendants -- the blessed line of Shem and not the cursed line of Ham.

God's purpose for Abraham and his posterity would not be thwarted. The Lord had given Eleazer favor to find Rebekah, in turn Eleazer wanted to ensure his precious cargo made it to their destination.

There is so much to learn from this servant's posture and stature, but let it suffice to say, *"The steps of a man are ordered by the LORD who takes delight in his journey" (Psalm 37:23 BSB).*

Watch what happens when Isaac and Rebekah finally meet. God had also prepared Isaac's heart and caused him to be at the right place at the right time. Isaac went out to the fields to meditate, meaning that he too had been praying and was expectant.

⁶²"Now Isaac had come from Beer Lahai Roi, for he was living in the Negev. ⁶³ He went out to the field one evening to meditate,[¹] and as he looked up, he saw camels approaching. ⁶⁴ Rebekah also looked up and saw Isaac. She got down from her camel ⁶⁵ and asked the servant, 'Who is that man in the field coming to meet us?' 'He is my master,' the servant answered. So, she took her veil and covered herself. ⁶⁶ "Then the servant told Isaac all he had done. ⁶⁷ Isaac brought her into the tent of his mother Sarah, and he married Rebekah. So, she became his wife, and he loved her; and Isaac was comforted after his mother's death."

What a magnificent love story! It holds the best ingredients for a love affair including intrigue, expectation, faith, prayer, meditation, and more prayer. Most important is to see the faithfulness of our God.

I believe that there are couples that unite for Kingdom Purpose such as with King Xerxes, and Esther (Hadassah was her Jewish name which means 'myrtle'. The myrtle tree in Hebrew is symbolic not only for 'peace', but also for 'justice').

I like to refer to those unions as having everlasting *Kingdom Ramifications*. Esther, (Hadassah) hid her Jewish identity from the King until the wicked Haman plotted to annihilate the Jews. This is when Esther rose to bring justice and peace to save her people. Her uncle Mordecai said, *"'Who knows, perhaps you were made Queen instead of Vashti for a time such as this!'"* (Esther 4:14b).

What does your marriage or desire to marry signify for you? Is it just a union for progeny or is it for Kingdom Purpose? You might have never heard anything like this, and you may even think I'm a bit in the left field, but I promise you, this is wisdom.

From Humble Beginnings

The trajectory of my life would have changed if not for the diligence of my mom and auntie who were concerned about my welfare and well-being. To think, had I not obeyed these matriarchs, God's purpose for my life would NOT have been fulfilled. Therefore, I do not shrink back when advising younger generations in matters of the heart.

My mom and aunt's own story of love and betrayal are interesting enough and portray strong, determined women with great courage.

Mom grew up in rural Starkville, Mississippi. When mom was still in High School, she fell pregnant. Her father was so upset, he grabbed his shotgun with the intention to shoot and kill the culprit. As God would have it, circumstances occurred to prevent this perilous tragedy from occurring.

Therefore, my mom had her first son out of wedlock. My father who was from Alabama, had lived a tough life. He had dropped out of school at the age of 13 to care for his mother and two sisters, and he grew up with a sense of responsibility that many young people his age were not aware of.

Dad married early, had two sons and life was good. Unfortunately, his wife was diagnosed with cancer and things went very quickly after that. She died, leaving dad with two sons to raise. Grieved and sorrowful, dad returned to work. He mentioned to a colleague and friend about his troubles and the colleague told my dad, not to worry. He believed he had a solution – to introduce dad to his girl-friend's classmate.

The day finally dawned for dad to meet mom. Arthur had put the plan into place. Upon arriving in Mississippi, he and my dad went straight to Arthur's girl-friend's place where it had been arranged for dad to meet mom. *"She was pretty and nice enough."* He thought to himself. *"But would she be able to take care of his sons and run the farm?"* He had wondered.

It turned out mom was somewhat quiet. Dad did not beat around the bush telling her his story from the beginning.

No sparks flew during this meeting. Dad simply told mom he had land to tend and two sons to raise. He asked her to come back with him to Alabama, and she agreed.

Mom's *dowry* consisted of a cow named Brenda and a *trunk with quilts and her keepsakes*. For the second time in a row concerning my mother's boyfriends, Grandpa went for his gun. Dad stood his ground and so did Mom. She told her father that she wanted to go with dad and to take her dowry with her! Now it took courage for a young woman of twenty-two to make such a radical decision, dad was twelve years her senior. But mom was determined and knew what she wanted in life. My siblings and I are so thankful for our upbringing and our parents.

When I think back on our childhood and how we were raised, I am so grateful to God to have been born in a Godly home with such hard-working and God-fearing parents. I have eight siblings and we never heard mom or dad arguing about anything. We never lacked, we always had just enough.

We grew up on a 40-acre farm with an orchard of lush green apple, pear, peach, and lemon trees. Wild, delicious muscadines were plentiful and plump over-ripe plums falling from their trees were scattered about the property.

The scent of freshly cut watermelon, cucumber and tomatoes would tantalize one's senses, beckoning to be devoured.

We mostly only ate from the land. Mom's cow Brenda produced enough milk for mom to churn to make buttermilk, fresh butter, and sweet milk. Behind the farmhouse was a chicken coup where our hens laid fresh farm eggs daily. There was a vegetable garden where mom grew string beans, okra, tomatoes, collard greens and other luscious vegetables. Mom would 'can' (a process using steam and an apparatus) the vegetables to be used during winter, to make scrumptious vegetable soup. This, eaten with large squares of warm buttered cornbread would carry us throughout the winter months.

Occasionally, dad would go hunting and catch squirrels or on rare occasions, deer to eat. This he would do under the thick cover of the night with only the stars to wink at him as if to say, *'Well done in taking good care of your family.'* When hunting season was over dad would wear a light strapped to his forehead, only switching it on when necessary. He knew the land like the back of his hand and knew where he had laid every trap. Once he had spotted his prey and nailed it with a single shot, he would mark the place, then return home to get mom to assist him in pulling the deer to the house. Somehow the two of them managed this daunting task. Mom would have the animal slaughtered by morning, meat hung in the smoke house and the carcass buried. Though she had only a few hours of sleep, mom would make breakfast for us children and be ready for a full day's work of washing, cleaning, and farmhouse chores. There was never a dull nor idle moment on the farm!

Hog killing day, (whereby a hog would be slaughtered), would take place only once or twice a year. Every part of the hog would be utilized including the skin which was deep fried, and its intestines made into chitlins, a southern delicacy. Nothing was wasted. Our close relatives would come and take part in this glorious provision of food.

We had a delightful childhood romping around in the woods, having each other and silk from our corn crop to play with, for dolls. I used to be embarrassed about living on a farm since we worked so hard throughout the fall, harvesting our corn and cotton crops and throughout the spring planting. There was never time for foot-ball games, extra-curricular school activities or visiting friends in town. Our entire life revolved around the farm.

It was not until I was in my thirties that I was able to see my early years from a grown-up perspective. What a rich childhood we truly had! Dad taught us the principles of arduous work, opened an account for each one of us children who wanted it at twelve years of age and taught us how to save our money. We did odd jobs such as cutting grass for the white people down the road or the rich people in town. Dad allowed us to keep part of the money and deposit it in the bank. He taught us the importance of paying one's bills on time and having good credit. Dad was well respected in the rural community as well as in town. He was a Sunday School teacher and never failed to take us to church.

Dad worked so hard and long in his life that his health failed him. He smoked until the day he died, which also wreaked havoc on his body. When our sweet papa had a heart attack in his fifties, I can remember the siren of the ambulance as if it were yesterday. We children gathered around him and cried until we were pulled away so EMS (Emergency Medical Services) could use their life saving equipment to work on him. We clung together, hugging one another, and cried thinking we had lost our father and we were all sorely distraught.

Thankfully, dad survived that heart-attack, but his health continued to decline. He recounted a story to us children of how he had seen his spirit leave his physical body and travel down a tunnel towards a bright light. His soul longed to be embraced by that light, engulfed into that cloud of pure light never to return to earth again. Yet his heart said, '*STOP*', because he had not properly prepared our mother or left the farm in good shape for her to take over. He decided to make a plea bargain with God. He asked the Lord to allow him to return to earth and carry out what his heart desired.

Dad did not go back on his word. As soon as he left hospital and was able, he attempted to teach mom independence. He began by training her how to drive. But after she ran into the mailbox and into the ditch, she was so discouraged she gave up on driving lessons. Next, he helped her to find a sitting job in the city and drove her back and forth. Dad tied up loose ends on the farm so that mom would be able to manage after he was no longer around.

Dad arranged for his funeral and even wanted to choose his casket, but his health didn't allow him to climb the stairs of the funeral home. Dad's health was stable throughout this time. We children coerced him into having surgery. We reassured him that he would come out fine, and he did. Dad's recuperation was miraculous. The doctor told him that smoking would be the death of him, and he said, '*So be it*' for this seemed to be the one bad habit that gave him such pleasure in life, he didn't care to kick. He no longer had an appetite therefore did not relish eating or drinking. Mom was diligent to prepare a soft diet which he took no delight in. He longed for the country food fare that he was used to eating but was no longer good for his condition, besides, he couldn't keep it down anyway.

On one occasion, dad had asked mom to assist him to the back porch where he could sit and look over the land. He allowed his eyes to rove over the many acres of corn which he had worked long and hard to procure the land. No doubt his mind reminisced over the extremely hard years of work which produced crop after crop every year. He thought of how at long last he went to the courthouse, signed, and possessed this farmland that would now be a legacy and an inheritance for his wife and children. He allowed his eyes to wander beyond the fields to the creek where he had hunted deer, squirrels and fished to help sustain his family.

Dad looked around the house that he had built with his own hands and with help from family members. A few years earlier, he had earned enough money from his crops to add an additional two large bedrooms and inside bathroom for the family. The girl's room had a fireplace that would heat up the front of the house. He blinked his eyes as tears glistened from the thought of it all. After his eyes got a fill of the works of his hands, he sighed. Mom said dad seemed satisfied that his days on earth had accomplished much, he returned to bed to retire for the night; this short walk had exhausted him.

On one fateful day when dad was recuperating in bed, our youngest brother, Archie was trying to mow the lawn but ran out of gas. As frail and poorly as dad was, he got out of bed, went outside, and showed our brother how to *siphon* gas from his truck. This was a process whereby you used a tube to *suck* the gas into a container before pouring it into the lawn mower. Dad was so weak he fell to the ground and had to be helped back inside. Later he was taken to hospital and never recovered.

God held up His part of the bargain and dad his. Mom was able to keep up with just a vegetable crop on the farm and went to work in town to her sitting job. With her meager salary, she managed to never get behind on any of the bills and to take care of my younger brother and sister till they went off to college. My youngest sister Betty is an RN (registered nurse) and my brother Archie is a teacher. We marvel at the goodness of God.

And for my aunt – hers was a story of betrayal. In her eighties, she maintained a vibrant lifestyle and still courted. She loved to watch wrestling matches on T.V., eat KFC, play Chinese checkers, and absolutely loved to put on airs. When dad would take her to town, she would dress in her very best, and saunter across the street to the bank, back straight and bust upright. She spoke in hushed soft tones in excellent proper English. She used to love to correct our grammar as children.

Aunt Annie gained her independence from a failed marriage in her younger years. The story goes that she used to go to the home of her husband's mistress and *pick a fight*. Her husband would be so embarrassed and ashamed, but my aunt did not care. She continued to make his life miserable until he came home, then she would be as sweet as pie. I can just hear her calling his name saying, "Sammy, what would you like to eat?"

My mother and aunt had earned their rights as **matriarchs** in our family. I would not dare question their integrity because I knew their experience dictated their actions.

Oddly, my mom only started participating in Church once my father passed. Like so many other things, we children never questioned our parents about these things. I figured she was just too busy on the farm. Aunt Annie got my mom to participate in going to singing events at various churches; now that was a fashion show of hats! Mom became a member of the choir and after helping on the church's hospitality team, she became the Director of Hospitality. Mom became more active within the community and even traveled with the church bus to Washington DC, Atlanta Ga, and other places. For many years, my husband and I had tried to get mom to visit Africa with us. She always said that she would come one day but was afraid to fly. Each year we came home, she would take road trips with us to California, Arizona, Florida, Detroit but Africa seemed just too far for her to go.

In 2006, Clement told mom that her ticket was purchased for the trip and all she needed was her passport! He coerced mom at 74 years of age into taking 16 flights to visit us in Nigeria! We stopped over in France where our twins had been attending school in Bordeaux. There my mom dined in the famous wine orchards of St. Emillion. She loved traveling and could not believe it had taken her this long to decide to go abroad!

Only in Paris airport we had a slight mishap with getting her off the flight. She had been assisted by wheelchair and taken to another gate! She was displaced from us for almost an entire day! We missed our connecting flights, but Clement did his best to go from one section of the airport to another and finally relocated her! Something our airline did little to assist us with! My mom had not been afraid and said she was *'lost with others her age'*! She had been pampered and was laughing and talking when Clement found her. Not understanding the language had not perturbed her one iota! She had called our brother Tommie to let him know that she was lost in the airport. He had reassured her that we were seasoned travelers, and she would soon be found, not to worry!

In no way did this unfortunate occurrence dampen mom's spirits. She proved to be a perfect traveler and never complained about anything. She even enjoyed the airplane food and slept during the long flights. Arriving in Nigeria, she was amazed at the change of terrain from France. It had been raining and was the monsoon season. There was dense fog that prevented airplanes from flying therefore we had to hop on the bus from Lagos to Port Harcourt which was another 12 hours before making it home! Mom took it all in stride.

She was spoiled royally in Nigeria. She was invited by our friends to restaurants and to their homes. Mom enjoyed taking Olivier, our grandson to kindergarten daily. The long walk was good for her legs, and she lost weight! I invited the braider and tailor home. We fashioned African clothing for her and had her hair braided. What a glorious time we all had but mom pined to get back home to church, choir and her weekly schedule of attending community activities in the center with her neighbors and friends. She spoke to them daily on the phone. She especially missed church and singing in the choir. So, Clement took her back before her planned date. In hindsight, this was a wise decision as a week later, a bomb had been planted on the premises and our entire camp had to be evacuated!

I owe these two steadfast **matriarchs** much for their guidance in my life and for whom I have become today. It is God who is Alpha and Omega, He sees our beginning and our end. Our days are crafted in His hands. He knows the plans that He has for each one of our lives, plans not to harm us but to give us hope and a future (Jeremiah 29:11). The Lord had to remind me of that Scripture fifteen years ago when I was passing by a '*road less traveled by*' in my life. Before the problem even began, God had me fast and gave me Jeremiah 29:11 as a Rhema Word, therefore when problems arose, I remembered God's promise and *stood still to see His salvation*. Again, my mom was key in helping me to navigate the stormy waters. My auntie had already gone to be with the Lord.

Too much godless television, movies and the lot have contaminated the minds of our children. The Bible says clearly for the older women to guide the young.

Titus 2:4-6 NLV
4 "Older women are to teach the young women to love their husbands and children. 5 They are to teach them to think before they act, to be pure, to be workers at home, to be kind, and to obey their own husbands. In this way, the Word of God is honored. 6 Also teach young men to be wise."

I am NEVER apologetic to those who do not understand this element of my role as a '*Sage Femme*'. As the idiom goes, *The proof of the pudding is in the eating*! The longevity of this couple – Joseph and Katrina – their lifestyle and love for one another has proven that their destinies were intertwined. Anyone who knows them recognizes their compatibility. They are renewing their wedding vows this week after 20 years of marriage.

All the Lord's promises are '*Yes*' and '*Amen*'. *The Sacred Words of A 'Sage Femme'* is all about Isaiah 49:22 NIV,

22 "This is what the Sovereign Lord says:
'See, I will beckon to the nations,
   I will lift up my banner to the peoples;
they will bring your sons in their arms
   and carry your daughters on their hips.'"

The Lord has brought many spiritual sons and daughters from many different nations. I have had the honor of mentoring them, praying for them, loving them and being a part of the miracle God wrought in them.

God has an uncanny sense of humor in that he blessed me with a gift to pray for those seeking the fruit of the womb. This has happened to those that are believers as well as non-believers. God is sovereign and He has had the last say in my life and ministry. I honor Him and hearken to His voice and His voice alone.

I have accepted my role as a spiritual mother as an honor bestowed upon me by Abba. It has been sometimes a tumultuous road but mostly an enjoyable one. The spiritual children I have had the privilege of assisting in their lives, have made all the difference in mine.

On the following pages, you will get the chance to read some of their stories which I like to refer to as '*Re-Stories*' because God is a God of '*Second Chances.*' We get a chance to begin again and pick up the broken pieces of our lives. These stories may illicit joy, sadness and even anger due to the outcome of some, but these are the unscripted stories, the realities of some and their existence lived out on planet Earth.

You might find yourself on the faded pages of this journal, outside looking in and seeing yourself in the lives of one of these. God is faithful, Daughter. God is faithful, Son. His plans for you are good not evil and for an expected end (Jeremiah 29:11).

Just today, I spoke to one of my daughters in Italy. I will begin with her story as it is so like my own. I first met Nicole in Holland when she cycled approximately 786 miles from Italy to Holland! The sheer thought of someone being able to cycle that far left me speechless. Knowing only that fact about her, told me already that she was tenacious, a go-getter and a force to be reckoned with.

Every young girl dreams of marrying her Prince Charming. Nicole was no different. Nicole is most certainly over 6-foot tall, a gorgeous model, designer, actress. Most men would fall at her feet because of her beauty, yet Nicole had eyes for only one man. And she waited patiently for him. She waited for nearly 10 years for someone who was elusive. But she did not *wait in vain*, many lessons were learned along the way. Did God change his mind? Certainly not!

On the next pages you will read the story of this brunette beauty and how she found solace and peace in God's true plans for her life.

Nicole's Re-story, Italy
My Testimony

God Answers the Desires that he places in Our Heart

I met Rhonda in 2016; I had just finished Missions School and been on an epic prayer journey across Europe in response to three visions God had given me during my time as a student, where He called me to serve in Europe. During that trip, God put in my heart a strong desire to have a Spiritual Mother. I had been mentored by so many men over the years: pastors, small group leaders, evangelism coaches, prophets, the director of my seminary program -- were all wonderful spiritual fathers to me who forever impacted my life, but I wished there was a godly woman who was Spirit-filled in the gifts who I could learn from and be mentored by.

Little did I know, but God had begun to grow this strong desire in my heart because He had already prepared an answer to that prayer waiting at the end of that journey for me, and her marvelous name was Rhonda Dikoko. As soon as I stepped in the foot of her door, I felt like I was home, and in our powerful times of sharing and prayer that week, He confirmed that the connection was from Him, a treasured gift I will always be so thankful for.

Rhonda & Nicole during her first visit sitting on Rhonda's prayer bench

One of the beautiful ways that God used Rhonda over the next few years was to help guide and shepherd my heart in the journey of meeting my husband. I met Rhonda when I was 34 years old, wondering 'where in the world is this guy.' I had been on a hidden prayer journey with the Lord, because God had confirmed time and time again to pray for a specific man that He had prepared to be my husband. In the past we had dated very intensely with the intention of marriage, but at the end of that time I felt God clearly telling me to let him go, to give the relationship to God, as God wanted to take his heart on a journey of seeking Him and knowing Him fully.

A few years later, through numerous unbelievable and dramatic prophetic confirmations, signs, Scriptures, and clear words from people who knew nothing about the situation, He called me to begin praying for this man again as my future husband. Many times, over the next three years I had worried it was a mistake, and I gave it up again to God, but each time He confirmed it. Not only that, but I saw God specifically answering each prayer of those prayers, as He led him on a journey of Lordship, putting God first in his life above any other ambition, career, desire, and worldly temptations. I had dreams and even demonic encounters about the spiritual battle taking place and wasn't sure why God had put me in this role.

I could see how much this man was called to. I felt that he battled fear and unbelief to answer this calling, yet God had asked me to walk alongside him to fulfill a beautiful ministry the Lord had prepared for him. I sensed how proud Jesus was of him, even when the day came that he confessed that as much as he wanted to marry me and have children with me--there was no other woman for him---he felt like he had to die to all earthly desires to serve the Lord single-heartedly. It was painful, but I knew it was right, and trusted that it was part of the journey. I honored him for it.

A long walk of faith in single direction

As another year passed without a clear answer, I began to struggle with discouragement. My story seemed so different than everyone else's around me, and I often felt powerless and very alone in the process, until I met Rhonda. I had always dreamed of a beautiful fairytale romance and praying alone in my room for a man who at times said I was the love of his life that he never stopped thinking of me, and at other times cut me off completely and acted as if I was invisible – I felt hurt and confused.

After reading Rhonda's book about her grandson's restoration and seeing the faith that she had to speak and believe the Word of God regardless of any circumstance or human outlook, I began to understand how she was able to pray as she did, with utter determination and trust in God. Through Rhonda I was encouraged, built up, and strengthened to persist in prayer-- drawing my faith not from any human circumstance or response to prayer, but rather in the nature and character of God. As another intercessor friend reminded me one time, "Is your hope in a prophetic word or is your hope in God Almighty, Nicole?!?!"

If anyone knows Rhonda, they know she is a fervent woman of prayer. We've had many powerful and unique times of prayer together, where it felt like heavenly realities began to manifest around us. I remember one time praying with her in her home in The Hague, and we decided we would go to the sea as a prophetic act, casting away unbelief and doubt and declaring God's victorious promises over my life. As we decided to go, dark clouds gathered overhead. It looked like it might start raining at any moment. I asked her how far away the sea was, and maybe we should consider postponing.

"Do you want this victory or not?" was her response. She had a playlist of battle songs for worship, and we started out. Suddenly the wind began whipping around us, pushing us almost backwards, and fat drops were speckling the sidewalk around us. Even though I've always been an athlete, I was feeling so tired, cold, and overwhelmed, wondering if we would ever make it to the beach. "Are you sure we shouldn't turn back?" I asked her again. "Listen to this worship song, my daughter! It's perfect for you!" (In hindsight, this was the song played at our wedding)! She beamed as she commanded the rain to hold off until we were done. Though it seemed to be sprinkling all around us about to downpour, we both somehow arrived at the beachfront completely dry. As we stepped onto the sand, the clouds broke open and light flooded through gloriously, and we had a victory worship time of prayer. Neither of us were rained on at all as we completed our intercessory assignment for that day. I realized that this was an important picture for me to live and pray in the Spirit.

A Promise of Home, and a Family

In those years I began to see many fruitful promises and victories of God fulfilled in my life: creatively, in my career, in my relationships, as God opened doors for me to start a ministry for trafficked women, had me working in Hollywood films and the fashion industry, gave me the resources to launch my own company and also cleared the way for me to move to Europe, opening all the doors as he had promised me three years before in Africa.

When I moved to Italy, it was a complete faith journey for me, and within a few months, God even miraculously provided me with my dream housing, including incredible views of the countryside and downtown, a stone fireplace, and a river path nearby. After almost ten years of traveling the world doing various projects and itinerant ministry, He told me, "This is your home, this first year I will plant you, the next year you will live here with your husband and children." He told me to put down roots and prepare the home, trusting him for the husband that was nowhere in sight.

Finally, in that season, it seemed even the long-awaited relationship He had promised me began to bloom. Each week we met to spend time together, writing messages and texts daily. Finally, one afternoon walking on the beach together at dusk, he thanked me 'infinitely,' from the bottom of his heart for not giving up on him, no matter how he had treated me, when so many others had. A few weeks later after dinner in the countryside under the stars of early summer, he told me, 'There is no rush, Nicole' he said, "I've felt so frozen, so stuck, but the truth is we have all the time in the world to be together."

The Year of Silence

Then, as had happened so many times before, he completely cut me off. No answer, no reason, no response. "This is too much, Lord," my heart complained. "I can't go through this again! It's just not fair." I literally had no strength to go on, and I felt my heart becoming bitter. It was the prayers and encouragements from friends that sustained me during this time. Besides Rhonda, a friend added me to a group of more than 100 women who committed 90 days to prayer and fasting for their husband, led by a prophetic intercessor named Sarah. This sustained me all summer long.

That fall, I struggled with the level of loneliness, depression, and even despair that seemed to turn all my joys into doubts. Even though I had seen many prayers answered, I felt like I could barely walk forward anymore, and I felt so weak to every temptation of the enemy; it became hard for me to worship or to sense God's presence. I had a wonderful Christian roommate named Rae, who was a prayer warrior in the faith, and her friend Manu, a drummer with a deep heart for Jesus. Alone I felt like I had nothing but joining with others was different. The three of us had met just before I left for Indonesia, sharing so many insecurities, weaknesses, fears --- but God also revealed His true Heart in that moment. As I took Manu's hand in prayer, tears of compassion suddenly flooded down my face, along with many words about the abundance of God's love pouring out and realized how present and caring He truly was.

Manu said later that in that moment it felt like Jesus took his hand, and chains of bondage that he carried for more than a decade seemed to be falling off in that one moment of prayer. As I left for Indonesia to work with the safe house of women, God started to revive and strengthen me again, encouraging me forward in every way. In one of my afternoons off, Rhonda and I prayed together for the man that God had chosen to be my husband. As I walked along the beach, and again I saw a tremendous picture of spiritual warfare holding him in bondage, with so much confusion between true identity and false identity. I really felt like I could no longer even pray, I felt so hurt and rejected by the situation, but Rhonda stood in the gap for me. While Rhonda and I prayed for this future husband of mine, Manu and Rae and I prayed fervently for the broken marriage of a sister in Christ whose husband had betrayed and left her. The three of us began to pour out prayers for restoration and healing in the areas of marriages and redemption.

The White Dress

While on this trip for Indonesia, I was delving into the world of fashion, to begin to market our brand helping women escape from poverty and trafficking. I was in a designer boutique, looking at jewelry samples when out of the corner of my eye, I saw a silhouette of a long dress hanging on a rack among many others. "You need to buy that dress," I sensed the Holy Spirit telling me. I was busy with the thoughts of my business, and all that we were trying to accomplish that day, and I quickly brushed it aside. Again, I felt the same message go through my head, and I shook my head, "Why would I buy that dress?" I asked. "Because you're going to be married soon, and you'll need that dress." This time I think I laughed out-loud, and definitely shook my head "No" at what seemed to be my own total randomness. As I continued looking through jewelry samples, the elegantly dressed salesgirl interrupted me. "Excuse me," she said, "but I think that this dress is for you." In her hand, she held the dress that I had barely glimpsed from the rack. It was a long white soft cotton dress, piled with many layers of ruffles, big swooping sleeves, and a slit in the middle. It was definitely a statement piece. "What?" I asked, shocked. "Yes, she said, I'm sure it's your size. This dress is for you." I shook my head in disbelief. This was Indonesia where the majority were short, and I'm a 6ft. tall woman. Nothing in Indonesia is ever my size.

Too curious by this strange series of interactions, I headed to the changing room. It fit perfectly for my height and weight, and it was beautiful. "But God," I argued, "This is really pretty, but it's nothing like what I wanted for a wedding dress, anyway." It was simple and casual, with a slit going up the front. I had always loved the idea of a heavy satin vintage style dress, full of embroidery and lace. Finally, I paused to pray again, and surrendered my thoughts to Jesus. "Maybe I'm crazy, but I'd rather be obedient and wrong, than miss what you might have for me." I couldn't imagine what I would ever wear this dress to, and in the back of my mind, I figured in the worst-case scenario maybe I could sell it online.

My Heart Will Trust You Still

After a year of silence, I finally found out the truth. I had gotten back from Indonesia, and met the man I wanted to marry, in a cafe to talk. As I pulled up to park, I felt the Holy Spirit tell me, "He's going to tell you all about his girlfriend." For the next hour, he did exactly that. He had met a beautiful, fascinating girl, and was seriously in love with her. It was a strange moment for me. Had I been wrong all along? Had he met the one God had for him? How could my true husband ever pass me over like this, after so many years of sharing and caring? As he spoke more about her, I grew sad for him. She wasn't a Christian, she didn't want to ever get married, or have kids.

"But what about family?" I asked him. It had been his lifelong dream to have children and a family, one of the things that had been so important to both of us. "Well," he told me, "She might be pregnant. She's terrified, but I am so happy. I know we will work through this, and the rest will come in time." God's grace covered me so perfectly. I could see him, as I always had, and felt filled with love and admiration for the wonderful father he would be. I congratulated him with all my heart and honored the man he was. That afternoon I sat on my porch, swinging in the sunset, and worshiped God. I finally felt strangely free. The circumstances of doubt, and fear, and whatever God had for me seemed stripped away, and I just felt at peace to trust God, to celebrate that only He was good, and to rest in the fact that He loved me.

"Truly, only you know, Lord." My roommate Rae had written a beautiful song in those weeks, and she told me that it was actually written prophetically for me. 'Have a little faith, my friend.' I lay everything down before God. In the next few days, I processed my heart. I felt clearly that God showed me this was not the woman for him, and felt heartbroken tears come to my eyes that their relationship would bring so much sadness. At the same time, I was shocked to find that I still believed in him, and if it was God's leading for me to still marry this man, I believed that a greater freedom, and greater love would follow even this painful situation and feeling of betrayal.

At this point, I told God that He would have to speak in an unmistakably clear way to me, whether I could finally let go, or if He was still calling me to believe and pray that this was actually my husband, it would have to come from another person, without any doubt of me 'imagining' it. With my friend, I set this fleece before him, "Lord, if this is your will, have anyone in the world call me with a clear prophetic word about this situation, whether I am to let go completely and finally, or press in. It has to be perfectly clear without a shadow of doubt, and coming from someone else, not me.'

The Word of the Lord

The next day Rhonda called. She had been in the middle of two big moves, moving a home overseas and selling another home to move across the country. We had only spoken once that year when we prayed together in Indonesia. In the midst of all of this, she called me up to faithfully minister the Word of the Lord to me.

"My daughter," she spoke to me, "I just had to call and ask you, what's going on with the man we have been praying for to be your husband?" she asked. "Why?" I asked in astonishment, "Why do you ask?"

"Because I feel the Lord has been speaking to me about him, and I just had to call and ask what the situation is." Besides Rae, there was no one in the world that knew the conversation that had just taken place the day before. I would have accepted a prophetic word from anyone in the world, at this point, but I was so happy that God had chosen Rhonda, a woman that I trusted so well, and that had deeply prayed and believed with me for this marriage and seen the Word of the Lord so clearly active.

"Oh Rhonda," I breathed a sigh of relief, "Please tell me first what you feel God has been saying to you. Then I'll share what's happening."

Anoint your Horn with Oil

She said, "Look up Samuel 15:28-30. This is the Scripture that God gave me for him. I feel that God is displeased with him, and says to him, "The Lord has torn the kingdom of Israel from you today and has given it to your neighbor, who is better than you. Also, the Glory of Israel will not lie nor change His mind; for He is not a man, that He would change His mind." She said.

And to you, dear daughter, I feel that the Lord is speaking to you as the prophet Samuel, and he says, "How long are you going to mourn for Saul, since I have rejected him from being king over Israel? Fill your horn with oil and go; I will send you to Jesse the Bethlehemite, because I have chosen a king for Myself among his sons.'"

She said, "Nicole, I believe God is asking you to rise up, stop grieving for this man, and anoint your horn with oil, because God is bringing somebody else for you and he will be like David, a worshiper! It's time to open yourself and open your eyes to what God is about to do." I could not ask for a clearer word, from someone that I trusted more. With anyone else, I might have wondered if it was just human wisdom, 'Move on, girl!' But this was Rhonda, the woman who continued to pray long after doctors had given up all hope and had seen the sick and dying come back to life. I had marched with her through enough prayer sessions to know that 'giving up' was not in her vocabulary, it didn't exist in her realm of faith.

If this was the Word God was ushering me through, He had chosen someone I could trust completely to not react to circumstances or fleshly discouragement, but rather who had trained herself to walk out a faith of radical obedience. I then shared with Rhonda everything that had happened and asked her to please pray for me that I would have the grace to fully obey without fear or bitterness. She told me she would fast and pray for three days to seek God about this before confirming with me.

Blooming Ahead of its Time

During those three days of prayer and fasting, I asked God to take everything from me that was too hard for me to let go of, after so many years and dreams. As I poured over the chapters of Samuel for guidance and healing, I was so grateful and amazed at how specifically and strongly God was speaking to me. If this was the Scripture that applied to my situation, I hadn't been 'wrong' as I feared all along, neither had God capriciously 'changed his mind.' There was something that God was specifically doing in all of this, and I could trust that it was good.

In many ways Saul looked like the 'dream' king that Israel had longed for--- beautiful, tall, wealthy, strong. Saul was deeply loved by Samuel, and he was loved and anointed by God, even counted among the prophets -- yet there was another man that God had raised up for the future of Israel, to create a lasting legacy.

Despite the relief at having gotten a clear answer in Scripture, I realized I was filled with the sense of dread and fear that now I would have to start all over again from zero, like the marathon runner who is about to cross the finish line, and is told, "This was the wrong race, you have to go back and start on a different route, from the very beginning." I was feeling overwhelmed and discouraged, yet when I finally trusted God with my future, I saw another little miracle bloom in front of my eyes. A prophetic symbol that God had always used to speak to me about my marriage, was white roses.

On the balcony of my porch, I had planted a rosebush. It was a long, skinny stick with only a few branches of leaves at the top, and it had never bloomed. I had planted it as part of what I one day hoped would become a beautiful garden for the family God had promised he would give me in that home. On the third day of praying, two huge white roses suddenly bloomed side by side, nestled together in the porch light and giving off the sweetest perfume of honey.

I sensed God beautifully wiping away my fears that it would *not* be another eight-year process of waiting, but instead, it would be something that would seem to bloom overnight, fully formed. Besides the number 8 is a number of new beginnings.

As I surrendered all to God, I was filled with the sweet revelation that the journey I had been on---with all its ups and downs--- was now solely for Jesus. In the end it hadn't been about an earthly person, but about learning to trust my true lover....and despite all my weaknesses and failures, He never abandoned me. He was willing to meet me clearly and strongly, even in this moment of seeming disaster, and that was the sweetest fragrance of all.

Two white roses that bloomed on the porch

"An hour is coming and now is, when the true worshipers will worship the Father in spirit and truth." (John 4:23).

One of the things that most encouraged me through that difficult year was the worship nights that we had in our home. When the Bible talks about Abraham being the father of faith, it says he was able to maintain the faith through worship. Full of music, art, creativity, and sincerity, we gathered worshippers in our home who felt free to share testimonies, Scriptures, songs, prophetic acts, without fear of judgment or religiosity.

God had been working in all of our hearts that year, and a small group of friends from international backgrounds had been meeting and praying together in our home, seeking more of God's presence. I will never forget one of those special nights, I felt as if I had been met and seen by God, who is always in the details. As we planned one of the worship nights, we had one particular friend who we felt God really wanted to meet that day. We thought about inviting him but knew he was probably not in town.

In fact, when Rae invited him, he said he was on tour on the other side of Italy, but his car was parked in Bologna, and he would love to come by our house on his way back. I didn't know him well, but as we prepared for our worship service, God had me write out a specific prayer message for him. *"You are not alone, you are loved, this is your home."* We expected him to come very late at the end of the night, but suddenly God had me hurry to print out this message and tape it to the front door. Ten minutes after I had put it up, he walked in the door and exclaimed, *"I can't believe the message on your door. This is literally the answer to my heart's prayer today, as I was feeling so alone, so lost, so far away from any Christian that I know. I asked God, 'Please help me find a place with other believers, where I feel at home.'"*

All year I had painted, prayed, gardened, cleaned, and fixed this old house, believing the promise that God had spoken to me about it being my future home. Although I was still single, no husband or family in sight, these nights made me feel that God Himself was building our home, filling it with people who belonged to Him, and who loved Him, gathering up His children who had been scattered or lost in Italy along the way, and making us into a spiritual family.

First Glimpse

That night as our friend came into dinner, I had the feeling that Jesus was walking into our home and seeing each of the little details of love and care that I put into it.... and the intention behind it... from the candles to the flowers, to the plates, the colors and art I had created--- our friend Manu saw and celebrated every detail. All year I had felt invisible and ignored, and in this special moment, I felt like it was Jesus Himself coming in to smile and receiving each drop of love that I had put into this promise, almost like an inauguration of our home.

Another significant prophetic moment of the night was when I sensed Jesus wanting me to offer a perfumed bowl of water for our guest to wash his feet in. I didn't know him very well and thought he would probably think it was very strange for me to do this the first time he came to our home. I prepared it anyway and offered it to him during the worship time, sharing that I felt Jesus wanted to wash his feet tonight. At the end of the night, as we spoke of how God had met us in this week, Manu told us how when he went through times of deep discouragement and darkness, he used to make a bowl of water in his room and wash his feet in it, imagining that it was Jesus washing his feet, cleansing him, and loving him in his brokenness. It was something he had always done in private, no one else knew about it. Tonight, he couldn't believe that Jesus had specifically spoken to him in that way that meant so much to him.

At that time, I could never imagine that this man was actually my real-life husband, walking into my home for the first time in my life. I just remember being so touched by his sincerity, and thinking to myself, "Wow, I love listening to him speak, everything he says is so fresh, and sincere, and creative, I could listen to him all night." After that meeting in our house he later told his sister,

"Wow, tonight I met someone who was a picture of exactly the kind of woman I would want to marry."

During this period of knowing him, I had always seen him as a younger brother, even as we had been praying together all Spring while I was in Indonesia, as we interceded for his sister's marriage to be restored. It wasn't until Rhonda's words unlocked me to be open for God to do something new, that a few weeks later coming back from a road trip together with friends, I realized how attracted I was to this handsome man--- a wild worshiper, a sensitive and caring friend, and one of the most beautiful hearts of kindness I had ever seen, *"the largest diamond in the world."* Looking back, I realized I had written on the door, *"This is your home,"* and in fact that year it became his home.

Nicole & Manu having a laugh

Love Revolution

When God finally released me to meet my husband, Manu, it was like He gave him the secret combination code and keys to my heart. I felt so instantly known, and seen, and loved as I was, by this person who had just come into my life. I remember each one of our first dates, tears falling from both my eyes, and his, as we realized how carefully and lovingly God was answering both of our prayers and cries of our heart in important times of our life. Through so many pains and disappointments over the years, hardness and callousness had grown over some of the softest part of my heart. Through this process of courtship, God was showing me how precious and important those soft parts were to Him, and He wanted to heal and restore every one of those places that the enemy had tried his best to damage. Though Manu and I come from very different backgrounds, cultures, and lifestyle, and we are even opposites in so many ways, since the very beginning the words that came most natural to us to describe our connection was, *"heart of my heart."*

Since the first weeks of starting our relationship, it was very obvious to both of us that we would be married at some point in our life. At the time I was preparing to leave for six months in Indonesia, and then America, we considered having a long-distance relationship until we got back. Again, and again God seemed to be confirming, "Be married, do not wait, do not hesitate, do not be afraid." After everything I had been through, my breakthrough came after some inner healing sessions to overcome fears about marriage that I never even knew I had.

We took time to fast and pray apart, and God continued to confirm with steady urgency, and confirm it through some of our closest and most trusted prophetic friends, and of course, Rhonda. As soon as we decided to get married, it was like a bomb of opposition went off all around us. Though our closest friends and mentors strongly supported us, we started to face levels of persecution beyond normal human response. There were also many financial and logistical challenges that seemed impossible to get through, because of international paperwork, financial limitations, travel and time restrictions, to name a few.... we trusted God that if this was really the direction. He was calling us, He would open the way and even part the sea if need be.

We spent the next few weeks gathering dozens of documents to be translated and submitted to the Italian courts, often traveling back and forth between 3-4 cities a day working with the local questura offices. Everyone told us it would be impossible to be legally married sooner than nine months in Italy, they said the process can even take two years. Many offices were closed or refused to process me as a foreigner, yet God continued to encourage us and confirm with many signs that he was leading and smoothing the way.

Both of our families were completely supportive of us, and to me this seemed like one of the biggest miracles, since they knew so little of the other person, though they had both been praying for our spouses for years. Unfortunately, organizing something quickly that both of our families could be a part of would be impossible, and so I had to fully surrender to God the "dream wedding" I had always hoped for. If this was his timing for us, then I trusted that somehow it would be best. We had made a private exchange of vows before God in June as we waited for our paperwork to process, but there wasn't time, or money, or possibility to have a real wedding, so it seemed.

Marrying Jesus

Early that Summer, we had organized to go on a mission trip with my longtime mentor and pastor, Robby Dawkins. It was ten days of equipping Muslim leaders and refugees in gifts of the Holy Spirit and would take place in Turkey. As it worked out, he welcomed us on the trip and agreed to perform our Spiritual wedding while we were there. For us, it was a beautiful idea that filled us with joy. Although our friends and family wouldn't be there, it felt so meaningful to start our married life on a mission's trip together, surrounded by the people of God, blessed by one of the key spiritual fathers in my life, and in an atmosphere seeking the Holy Spirit in worship with believers from many nations, and the persecuted Church. We were both happy for the simplicity and purpose of the wedding.

"If only I had a nice dress to wear," I told Manu. Then suddenly I remembered the dress that the Holy Spirit had led me to buy a few months before. "It's better than nothing," I thought as I threw it in the bag along with a dark pantsuit for Manu. We left for Turkey excited to meet Robby and the team, not knowing if we would end up getting "*married*" in a refugee camp, a hotel lobby, or some random meeting room. As it turned out, our day off was Thursday, and Wednesday night our group decided to go to visit the historical cave where John encountered his vision of Jesus and wrote the book of Revelation. All afternoon they tried to arrange travel, but it seemed the only options involved 4-5 ferries and 18 hours of travel. We gave up, but then one of the leaders called some military connections he had and was able to charter a private yacht to take our entire team to the beautiful Greek Island of Patmos, the next morning.

Manu and I spent time praying that night, asking God to meet us and confirm us in our call to marriage. When we met again to share, it turned out that God had told us each three things. In fact, he told us both the exact same three things:

1. Never forget your first love, return to your first love like the church of Ephesus.
2. Tomorrow you are marrying me.
3. Manu needs to wear white tomorrow, not black.

This revelation would become so important to me in the next few years and months to come.

Jesus was telling me that the day I married Manu, he himself married me. Jesus is always loving, always faithful, and always the perfect husband. Though Manu and I are both far from perfect, we can trust that somehow Jesus chose us as His vessels through which He will manifest His covenant of perfect bridal love to us, and despite any circumstance or hardship, I can trust that His love is faithfully present with me and sustaining me. If Manu and I expect each other to be the perfect husband or wife, we will be disappointed, but I can always rely on Jesus to be that covering for me; not apart from our marriage, but actually within and through the marriage He chose for me. When Manu and I keep Him as our true love, needs and issues I don't even dare mention are taken care of, and everything else in our marriage begins to flourish.

Worthy of It All

We woke up before sunset to board the yacht and spent the first morning of our marriage watching the sun rise over the Aegean Sea. It felt like a beautiful dream, the start of a lifelong voyage filled with a wide blue sky, fresh wind, and deep waters that so many saints had sailed before us. The team was giddy with excitement for us to be married, and they gave us so many blessings and encouragements in the days before our wedding. A friend brought a package shipped from home with letters, gifts, and a pair of gold wedding shoes for me.

When we landed on Patmos, I stopped in a shop across from the harbor and we found white linen clothes for Manu and a pair of leather sandals. The girls from our team helped me pick a bouquet of flowers along the road, and we caught a cab up to the cave to pray. When our driver found out we were planning to get married that day, he said, "Leave everything to me, I know just the spot." As it turned out, one of our team members was a National Geographic photographer who was finishing up a documentary in Turkey. He knew my grandparents from decades before in Colombia, and he offered to take pictures and videos of our ceremony.

After visiting the cave, our cab driver hurried us to the top of the island. "Go into this restaurant to change," he told me, "I'm friends with the owner and he knows you're coming." Then he sent Manu, my pastor, and the photographer to the top of the hill. What I didn't realize until now, was that the dress that Jesus had picked out for me months before, was the absolute perfect dress for a summer wedding in Greece. Dozens of layers of soft cotton gathers billowed and tossed in the wind. The full sleeves felt like butterfly wings dancing in the island breeze and my long veil flew around me like a song of joy from the Holy Spirit. If I had searched all around the world, I don't think I could have found a more perfect dress for that moment, that Jesus had planned all along.

I did my hair and makeup in the restaurant, and as I stepped out into the cobblestone streets looking where everyone had gone up the road, the islanders came out of the doorways and windows to watch me and wave and cheer me on. Everything was painted white, and as I wound up the old road that curled up towards the church on the hill, I was laughing as so many strangers were cheering and clapping and waving for me. As I came up to the last steep steps leading up to the church, I caught the sound of beautiful singing.

Tears came to my eyes as I heard the praise song lifting to the skies, "*Worthy of it all, you are worthy of it all.*" I had been on such a long difficult road with Jesus, so many ups and downs over the last thirty years.... but here I was, covered in every way with the love and presence of my Jesus who had dressed me Himself with beautiful soft linens of gladness where before there had been despair. He was truly the one who was worthy of it all.

When I turned the corner, I was the one that gasped, because in front of my eyes was the most beautiful scene I could imagine --- a white church arching over a panoramic view of white islands floating over the waters, the blue Aegean Sea melting into the sky in every direction. There was Manu, standing next to Robby and both were smiling at me. It was one of the most joyful moments of my life, and I couldn't believe that Jesus had planned such a beautiful wedding for us, every detailed hand-picked by Him. I felt like one of His precious lilies of the field; not even many movie stars could have such a special wedding day as He had chosen for me, sailing back over the waters that afternoon into the sunset on a private yacht through the Greek islands, dancing with champagne and baklava, receiving prayers and blessing from the Body of Christ with so much joy and celebration.

Though I'd spent most of my life planning and dreaming of my own wedding day, and helping co-ordinate elaborate weddings for other people, Jesus surprised me with a more beautiful wedding than I could possibly have wished for.

Greek Wedding Photos

Greek Wedding Photos

A week after getting back from Patmos, our Italian paperwork miraculously came through on the very last day before the offices closed for Summer. That Monday, we received a call that there had been a wedding canceled, and if we still wanted to, we could have our Italian civil ceremony officiated that Friday afternoon, in the medieval castle of Formigine, my husband's birthplace. His parents were delighted to organize a family dinner party for us, filling up tables with flowers and candles and endless courses of incredible Italian food, far beyond what anybody was able to eat.

My friends from America happened to be flying in that same day. I picked them up from the airport and surprised them with the invitation to our Italian wedding feast that night. In the car, I finished sewing a long satin gown for myself, out of heavily embroidered vintage silk, and a matching medieval suit for Manu -- it truly was a Romeo and Juliet fairytale castle wedding with many of our dearest friends and family in Italy. Two weeks later, we left on a three-month honeymoon trip to the island of Nusa Penida in Indonesia, and our fourth wedding took place in Tucson, officiated by my spiritual mom, Rhonda Dikoko, surrounded again by friends and family in a million dollar Desert Villa, and a handmade vintage lace wedding dress.

When I handed my broken dreams over to God, He somehow gave me back the most beautiful dream of all, far beyond what I could have dreamed or imagined.

Italian Wedding

Tucson Wedding

God's Timing, not Ours

Though our wedding process felt so rushed in many ways and is probably not anything I would recommend to most people, we clearly felt that the urgency was something that had come from God, not our own preference or idea of *'the right way'* to do things. A year later when we arrived back in Italy and gave birth to our daughter a month prematurely, just weeks before Italy became the epicenter of global coronavirus pandemic, we realized the timing could literally have not been more perfect. We had just finished the last of our follow baby visits at the hospital when I entered lockdown with my husband and new baby in a beautiful home God had prepared for us.

I'll never know the exact reason why God so clearly urged us not to delay but get married immediately, but I know that if we had not obeyed but followed the traditional human wisdom to spend time getting to know each other, we might have not even been able to get married for two years, if at all. We definitely would never have gotten to enjoy traveling the world to remote islands on our honeymoon, celebrating our marriage with my family, or have our first daughter in normal hospital conditions. (As the pandemic started in March of 2020, our hospital would become the central care center for coronavirus patients.) So many times, we are frustrated when God's timing seems too slow, or too fast, but truly His timing is perfect.

A Fairy Tale Ending

Almost since I first started walking and talking, I was dreaming of a beautiful fairy tale wedding. As a little girl, my sisters and I would drape a towel over our heads as a veil and walk down the aisle together. There was something about the beauty, the romance, the mystery of that moment and the sense of journeying together that seemed to fill my heart even as a little girl. As I think about what the true meaning *'fairy tale wedding'*, I realize that it's found in the invitation of our truest Bridegroom, our first love.

"The Spirit of the Sovereign Lord is upon me, for the Lord has anointed me to bring good news to the poor. He has sent me to comfort the brokenhearted and to proclaim that captives will be released, and prisoners will be freed. He has sent me to tell those who mourn that the time of the Lord's favor has come, and with it, the day of God's anger against their enemies. To all who mourn in Israel, he will give a crown of beauty for ashes, a joyous blessing instead of mourning, festive praise instead of despair.
In their righteousness, they will be like great oaks that the Lord has planted for his own glory" (Isaiah 61:1-3 NLT).

When Manu and I met, we were full of brokenness and hurt, because of sin in the world, of others against us and because of our own sin. Both of us had cried out to God, even years before, asking Him to fully take our life, our desires, our weaknesses, our first love. In the moment that we met, both of us were even at a point of giving up, aware that unless God did a miracle, there really was no hope apart from Him. God covered us in His grace, and His love, and His beauty, even when we least deserved it. Our marriage was never perfect from the start, and neither was it ever perfect afterwards. Jesus meets us in our areas of sadness, captivity, and destruction, and His purpose for every area of our life is to turn it to blessing, beauty, and praise.

There is no addiction, no struggle, no weakness that is greater than His ability to love us, heal us, and cover us with His favor like a bridal veil in the wind. This to me is the fairy tale ending that Jesus wants to write in every area of our marriages, our lives, not just for our sake, but also so that as we grow into His righteousness, we can be a *'Planting of the Lord for the display of His glory'*. If we allow Him to continue to meet us in each of our areas of poverty, sadness, captivity, mourning, and despair, His promise will extend not only to us but as a legacy over our future families, and as a restoration of those lives that went before us, as His promise continues in Isaiah, *"They will rebuild the ancient ruins, repairing cities destroyed long ago. They will revive them, though they have been deserted for many generations"* (Isaiah 61:4 NIV).

Entering the Promised Land

As a single woman, the thought of being married always felt to me like the hope of finally entering the *'Promised Land'*. My years of being single had felt like 40 years wandering in the desert, being guided and provided for by God in so many supernatural ways and learning to trust Him. Finally, He had brought me to my own "land" and given me a home. I received many important lessons about this along the way, and how we have to rid our hearts of bitterness, grumbling and complaining, in order to cross into the Promised Land. During my first year of marriage, I re-read through the Bible, and realized for the first time what it actually meant to enter into the Promised Land. It wasn't a time to finally sit back and eat grapes on the beach of Galilee with a honeyed-wine cocktail.

Actually, entering into the land of promise was a time of courageous battle, victoriously conquering the *'giants'* of the land, through trust and close reliance on God's plan for our life. No marriage is perfect because no human is perfect. All of us have areas of life, our past, maybe our habits, mindsets, addictions, or cultural strongholds that are *'enemies'* of the kingdom of God. God does not want us to co-habit with these foreign cultures, to make peace with them, or to intermingle. When we get married, we sometimes become overwhelmed and afraid when we see the "*giants*" that seem to inhabit our spouse's land, but they are probably feeling the same way about the "*giants*" in our land.

The good news is that Jesus has already promised to give us victory over every enemy of our life, and of our husband's life. He, Himself is leading the way, and His purpose is to strengthen us and shape us into a people of God who will reflect His majesty, His rule, and His glory here on earth. Jesus, Himself is the "*Commander of Heaven's Armies*" fighting for us and making impossible victories easy…until we can grow to fully inhabit, to fulfill, and to enjoy every goodness and richness of Heaven's promise over our lives. The Israelites who left Egypt constantly feared that God "brought us here, only to die", but Jesus' promise for us is that He came so that we might have life, and life abundant as we trust Him in the process, even as it winds and twists steeply up paths we would have never imagined, sometimes difficult, sometimes painful, but often with views of His love so beautiful, that they take our breath away.

Nicole's wedding cake was made by her grandmother and decorated by me. My prayer and blessing over them in the USA with Nicole's family and closest friends present.

Recently below, Nicole, Manu and Bella announce a new edition to the family. Welcome Sky.

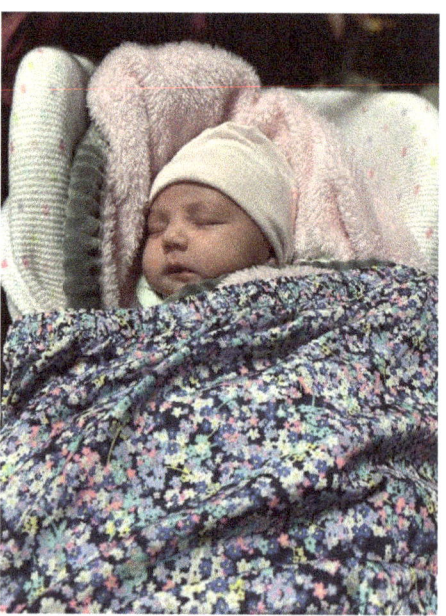

Gary's Re-story, USA
My Testimony – Soar like an Eagle

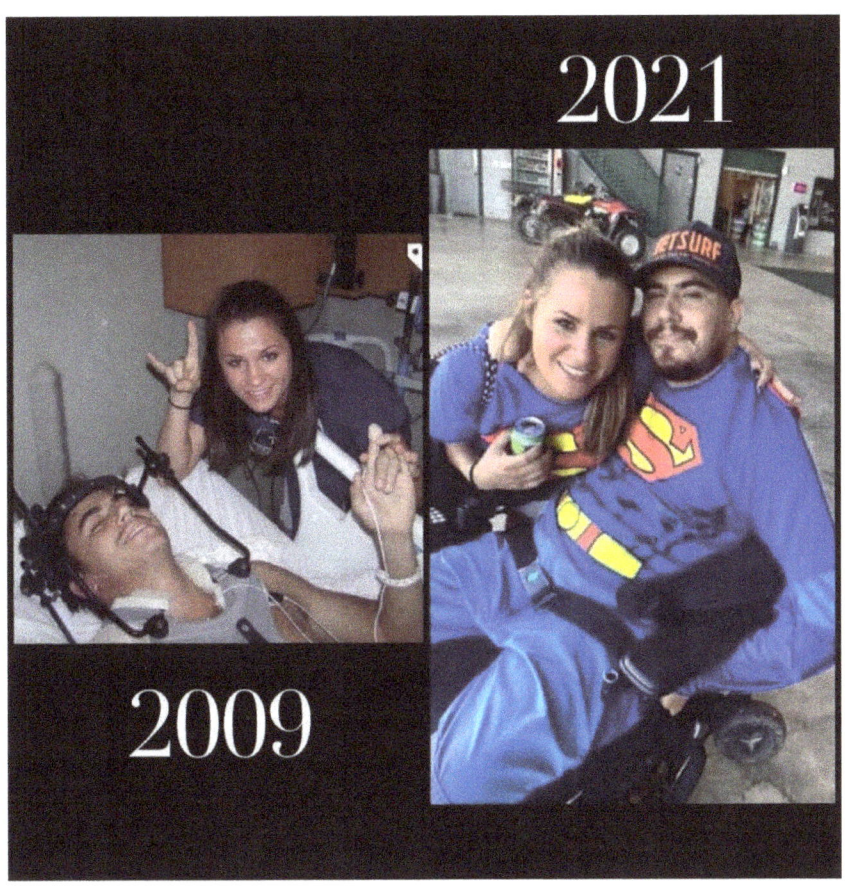

Gary met with an unfortunate accident which left him a quadriplegic at 21. Gary had earlier pronounced these words, "Nothing will stop me unless I'm paralyzed". Proverbs 18:23 NLT reads: *"The tongue can bring death or life, those who love to talk will reap the consequences."*

The Bible says in Mark 11:24 that you will have what you say. What you speak shapes your life. Be careful of the words that come out of your mouth.

This is what the Bible says about *Taming the Tongue*.

Taming the Tongue

¹"Not many of you should become teachers, my fellow believers, because you know that we who teach will be judged more strictly. ² We all stumble in many ways. Anyone who is never at fault in what they say is perfect, able to keep their whole body in check. ³ When we put bits into the mouths of horses to make them obey us, we can turn the whole animal. ⁴ Or take ships as an example. Although they are so large and are driven by strong winds, they are steered by a very small rudder wherever the pilot wants to go. ⁵ Likewise, the tongue is a small part of the body, but it makes great boasts. Consider what a great forest is set on fire by a small spark. ⁶ The tongue also is a fire, a world of evil among the parts of the body. It corrupts the whole body, sets the whole course of one's life on fire, and is itself set on fire by hell. ⁷ All kinds of animals, birds, reptiles and sea creatures are being tamed and have been tamed by mankind, ⁸ but no human being can tame the tongue. It is a restless evil, full of deadly poison.⁹ With the tongue we praise our Lord and Father, and with it we curse human beings, who have been made in God's likeness. ¹⁰ Out of the same mouth come praise and cursing. My brothers and sisters, this should not be. ¹¹ Can both fresh water and saltwater flow from the same spring? ¹² My brothers and sisters, can a fig tree bear olives, or a grapevine bear figs? Neither can a salt spring produce fresh water." (James 3:1-12 NIV).

Gary has paid a high price for this lesson well learned. He is an Exhorter and encourages people daily, he does motivational speeches and is a man who loves the Lord and who is learning to put God first. His tongue is being used for the expansion of God's Kingdom and he has been instrumental in pushing me forward in ministry, to have a higher yet attainable goal. According to him, it all has to do with your vision.

Gary always sees BIG and expansion in everything he does! Once he told me, he would love to see me on TBN! TBN (Trinity Broadcasting Network) is an international Christian-based broadcast television network and the world's largest religious network. I thought he was joking because I did not see myself as TBN material. TBN is for gigantic ministries and silver-tongued men and women of God. Gary didn't laugh with me but went on to speak about his vision and possibilities for my ministry. I don't mention this because I would like to be on Trinity Broadcasting Network, but to show you what can happen when you take your limits off God!

Despite of being paralyzed, Gary continues to soar like an eagle! He is the most positive and interesting person you will ever meet. Speaking with him on the phone or over zoom, no-one would ever know he was quadriplegic, unless he told you. Gary loves traveling, he's jumped out of a plane twice, he does fund-raisers, builds websites, and runs his own marketing company.

Gary goes on dates, has relationships, and lives as 'normal' as someone in his predicament can live. Most importantly, Gary gives to others and his heart is for other people to soar like an eagle just as he tries to do daily. Gary's faith is what enables him to get through every minute of the day.

When I met Gary, he felt 'stuck' in a relationship. I helped him see that he needed to 'let go and let God'. Christmas 2019, Gary attended Sunday service with my family and me, and online thereafter.

Slowly, Gary's mindset changed, and we played a newlywed game together to help with his paradigm shift. Gary has not yet found the girl of his dreams, however through my coaching, prayers and counseling he has exited the love triangle and is now available to receive what God has to offer him.

(Reference: www.sociableoutreach.com)

www.Fb.com/HelpHopeLiveGaryBolton

✻✻✻

Forgiveness

It occurred to me that I had hurt a spiritual son and even a spiritual daughter due to a misunderstanding, distance, and a pre-arranged rendezvous, with a promise of a future discussion which never occurred, because the spouse passed away. In Heaven none of these things will matter, but still I am writing this testimony to help somebody while they are still living, to make amends as soon as they are aware dissension has occurred.

My husband had made a call to this young man as he did occasionally. I was driving so my husband put the caller on speaker. I greeted our dear friend and my spiritual son, his response shocked me. His voice held hurt, regret, and pain. I realized at that moment that I had inadvertently caused a rift in our relationship because of a misunderstanding with his deceased spouse. I knew I needed to release the husband, and I did so via a zoom call which lasted around two hours.

Forgiveness is such a blessing to our souls. Not only for those who are forgiven but also those who forgive. It frees us. God never intended us to be bound by unforgiveness. It is a blessing-blocker which prevents the goodies of Heaven from falling afresh on us. We should be readily available to forgive on a whim and keep moving forward to the prize in which God has called us.

Personal Reflections

_____

_____

_____

_____

_____

David and Jody Jackson's Re-story, USA

As told to Rhonda Dikoko – The Power of Forgiveness

The Jackson Family lifting Brian after he graduated from Law School. Brian is the son who encouraged his dad to forgive the perpetrator.

David stood in the backyard gazing up at John David's tree he had planted only a few years back. David had planted an oak tree for every member of his family. He allowed his thoughts to take him back to the day he purchased the trees, bought fish as fertilizer, and watched his children water their tender shoots. John David, the eldest of the two used to fight with his sister Suzanne over whose tree was the tallest. Today his tree stood almost the same height as the other three. But John David would never see his tree grow up, he would never graduate from High School or go to college. His tender young life had been snatched away in a freak gun accident.

David sobbed softly to himself as the guests mingled in his home talking quietly amongst themselves, in hope of bringing comfort to his family by their presence. But David wanted none of it. He preferred standing in the backyard in the rain to being cramped up in the house with a bunch of folks who understood nothing of his family's pain and turmoil, brought on by the loss of their son.

For the first time in his life, David felt utterly helpless and alone, unable to do anything to remedy the situation. He felt doomed to a life of despair and hopelessness. "Senseless!" David muttered under his voice, intense anger taking hold of his entire being. The death of his son did not make any sense to him. How could a loving God be so cruel? He didn't want to go back into the house with the crowd, he preferred to be outside alone in the cold winter temperature, rather than enjoy the warmth of the hearth and company inside.

David looked intensely at his deceased child's tree, startled to find a dove peering back at him! Normally doves would take flight at the mildest of noise but not this dove. He sat perched in John David's tree staring straight at him!

David took a step towards the tree, but the dove didn't even flinch. David kept vigil each day watching the tree, till one day he discovered there was a nest with 2 eggs! Somehow this sign brought great comfort to him, as he believed in his heart John David was with the Lord. He also felt the two eggs meant God would bless him with two more children, and He did! David and his wife Jody had two more sons!

One of those sons, Brian, grew up to become a lawyer. He had grown up hearing about his brother's death and wanted to do research on the boy who had shot him. He knew a monument had been erected at John David's school in memory of his life, but what of the young man who had taken his brother's life? What Brian discovered was not surprising. The young man had had a turbulent childhood, drifting in and out of trouble. He later married and had children but seemed to barely be surviving in life. Brian felt for this young man and told his father he believed strongly in the power of forgiveness. He told his dad he should visit the shooter and release him from the debt of murder that must surely be weighing him down.

A year had gone by since David had been told this by his youngest son, Brian, yet he had taken no step towards restitution of the killer's own life. Thirty years had gone by since his son's death and David and his family had lived successful lives. He felt as though he had forgiven the young man who terminated his son's life but had not properly released him. Now he was ready to do so. He planned to gather his family, even bring his daughter from Seattle, and go to visit the young man. He asked me to pray a prayer over him and his family.

Forgiveness can lead to feelings of understanding, empathy, and compassion for the one who hurt you. Forgiveness doesn't mean forgetting or excusing the harm done to you or making up with the person who caused the harm. Forgiveness brings a kind of peace that helps you go on with life, in addition to releasing the guilty person(s).

Holding on to unforgiveness is a blessing-blocker in your life. Look at what Jesus says in Matthew 18:18-22 NIV –

[19] "'Again, truly I tell you that if two of you on earth agree about anything they ask for, it will be done for them by my Father in heaven. [20] For where two or three gather in my name, there am I with them.'
[21]Then Peter came to Jesus and asked, 'Lord, how many times shall I forgive my brother or sister who sins against me? Up to seven times?'
[22] Jesus answered, 'I tell you, not seven times, but seventy-seven times.'"

In Verse 19 Jesus tells us how to get our prayers answered. In the next breath he reiterates the exact same thing, letting us know that we should extend unlimited grace to those who wrong us, because we ourselves have been recipients of the grace of God.

In the Bible, the Greek word translated **"forgiveness", literally means "to let go," as when a person does not demand payment for a debt**. Jesus used this comparison when he taught his followers to pray: *"Forgive us our sins, for we ourselves also forgive everyone who is in debt to us"* (Luke 11:4 NIV).

Pray: Lord, forgive me of my sins and I also forgive and release _____ for doing wrong to me. Today, I choose to forgive and to let go, in Jesus' Mighty Name, Amen.

David and his family's story was shared with his permission, in the hopes of helping others get through their pain.

Personal Reflections

_____

_____

_____

_____

_____

Treasury of Scripture – Words of Wisdom

His Yoke is easy, His Burden is light

This heavenly journey is not for the faint at heart but for the swift and those who are not heavy laden in their spirits! This is what Jesus beckons us to do in Matthew 11:28-30 NIV,

²⁸ "'Come to me, all you who are weary and burdened, and I will give you rest. ²⁹ Take my yoke upon you and learn from me, for I am gentle and humble in heart, and you will find rest for your souls. ³⁰ For my yoke is easy and my burden is light.'"

This is the verse of Scripture that we governed Oasis Bible Study by, for the almost seven years I led the ladies in Kuala Lumpur, Malaysia and it continues up until now!

It is a personalized invitation from Jesus our Savior to come unto Him, ALL who are weary and burdened. That ALL encompasses everyone. Every nationality, religion, creed, and tongue. No-one has been left out or forgotten due to their status in life. ALL means ALL. Selah. Jesus is offering HIS REST. The '**rest of Jesus**' is being able to sleep through the storms of life! The '**rest of Jesus**' is not being concerned about what to eat or drink or with what we shall be clothed. The '**rest of the Father**' is knowing that He cares for you and will not forsake you. David says it like this in Psalms 37:25 NIV:

"I was young and now I am old, but I have NEVER seen the righteous forsaken or his young begging bread."

Faith's Re-Story, Nigeria
My Testimony

A song of ascents. *"When the Lord restored the fortunes of Zion, we were like those who dreamed."* (Psalms 126:1 NIV).

This Psalm echoed in my spirit after I had attended a Women's Conference in Nigeria. I had been a guest speaker as well as the Mistress of Ceremony for the event. I had been living in The Hague and working full time when I received the invite to travel for the conference.

It is a well-known fact that I seldom sleep on flights especially when I have meetings planned. I usually study the Word and prepare during the flight. This occasion was no different.

The organizer, Dr Bero (who is one of my best friends and a leading doctor in Lagos, Nigeria) and I sat in the car outside the venue where the event was being held. She was holding a small box of scriptures which contained promises from the Bible. She held her precious commodity tight to her bosom and suggested in a raspy voice, "Let's choose a promise before the conference begins".

"Good idea," I replied thinking to myself how I needed all the blessings I could get from the Lord to get through that evening. Not only was I jet-lagged but I also felt ill prepared for the event.

Arriving at the venue, the place was jam-packed. Dr. Bero asked my opinion on the order of the service. Left up to me, no dinner would have been served, however; the plan was already set in place. I suggested we have dinner near the end of the event to allow people to focus on the spiritual food (Word of God) rather than the physical.

The fire of the Holy Spirit was present. From the moment I introduced the first speaker, she took the microphone and prophesied to me that I would minister to people of all different nationalities, *yellow, white, black and red.* I marveled at her words because yellow referred to Asian. I had always had a desire to live in Asia. My husband had thought it an impossibility due to job complications or technicalities. Yet and still, I had secretly prayed to move there knowing God could cut all the red tape.

I anticipated that it would be a Spirit filled evening. The atmosphere was charged and surprisingly the fatigue I had previously felt seemingly vanished into thin air upon entrance into the venue. I could sense the place had been bathed in prayer as the presence of God was tangible. Every speaker thereafter ministered in the exact same vein gaining momentum with each Minister.

I was the last to speak therefore no formal introduction was needed   As the Lord would have it, prophecy and words of knowledge spilled forth. I singled out one woman who I will refer to as Faith and told her she would have a child. I found out much later this was a medical impossibility. Not only was Faith 49 years of age but she had been married for almost 15 years and had never been pregnant nor had a late cycle. I shook my head wondering what possessed me to say those words to her. The unction of the Holy Spirit. She had faith to believe that this was her time for reaping the harvest she had sowed tears for!

I focused my attention back to Faith and her husband who were sitting across from me after the service. They had sought me out for additional prayers. Suddenly, I remembered the promise I had randomly chosen from the little box Dr Bero had held so tightly prior to service!

To my closest recollection the scripture was either Matthew 24:35 NIV, *"Heaven and earth will pass away, but my words will never pass away."* Or 1 Samuel 3:19 NIV, *"And Samuel grew, and the Lord was with him, and did let none of his words fall to the ground."*

(I usually memorize scripture; it has been several years now so I'm unsure which one of the two it was).

Whichever verse it was, it gave me the confidence I needed to pray in faith for this couple despite their circumstances or my fatigue. Faith had also determined her years of infertility had ended. She locked her faith with mine and she signed the deal with God! She had planned on coming to The United Kingdom during Christmas therefore we planned to meet then.

She and I fasted during the Christmas holidays, she in the UK and I in Holland. We decided she would visit me to seal our prayers of agreement and to see a doctor which we did. The results were nothing short of a miracle from God.

Faith was small in stature with ageless features therefore could have easily been mistaken for someone in her late thirties. After examining Faith, The French doctor studied her demographics as well as her clinical information as he bobbed his head comically up and down peering at Faith then back at her report. Clearly, he appeared skeptical concerning her predicament due to her age and recommended to me in French to abort the baby (assuming it was a mistake).

I gestured to Faith to get dressed and we quickly thanked him, rushing from the office laughing like two teenage girls once we were outside. We located my car expediently, hopped inside locking the door behind us. We sat in silence for a moment before bursting into hysterical laughter again remembering the doctor's facial expression of alarm, mouth agape as we hurried past him into the cool, fresh night air.

Although the sky was dark, the stars were visibly twinkling to the melody of the trees which swayed in a dance to the fierce Northern wind. Everything about that evening seemed supernatural and surreal. Even time appeared to stand still. Our hilarious laughter ceased as abruptly as it had begun. We sobered at the realization of the magnitude of the blessing Father had bestowed upon us. Faith pulled her coat tightly across her small frame pressing her hand upon her flat tummy and began to glorify God in tongues and in song.

I prayed Psalm 126:1 NIV over her quite frequently after that: *"When the Lord restored the fortunes of Zion (Faith), we were like those who dreamed."* This resonated in her spirit.

This dear sister stayed with my family often during her pregnancy She had plans to return for her last trimester; however, we were packed and ready for our move to Malaysia by then! Remember my prophecy at that conference? The first speaker had prophesied that I would preach to black, red, yellow, and white people? It also came to pass!

Dr. Bero called to let me know she was in on our secret. "Rhondy, take photos of Faith's stomach because people will never believe Faith has given birth after this many years of infertility." She wisely advised. I promised I would. I also made Dr. Bero vow she would not divulge our secret until after the appointed time. Not even my family knew the truth!

Nigeria has the greatest number of multiple births in the world nevertheless, there is a stigmatism towards women who cannot conceive. Promptly, I took photos as proof of her pregnancy and sent them to Faith's husband and Dr. Bero as our witnesses of God's glory.

Later when Faith returned to Nigeria with her baby girl, a huge celebration was given on their behalf! A beautiful Thanksgiving service was organized unto the Lord which I was unable to attend because of our family's relocation to Malaysia. I was told streets were sequestered as people danced and celebrated Faith's wondrous blessing from the Lord!

"He settles the childless woman in her home as a happy mother of children." Praise the Lord, Psalms 113:9 NIV.

In that glorious conference, the Lord accomplished something for this dear Saint as well as for me. My dream to move to Malaysia came to fruition which led to my involvement with Oasis Ladies Bible Study! The Lord has marvelous plans for us, Dear Ones.

"For I know the plans I have for you, declares the lord. Plans to prosper you and not to harm you, plans to give you hope and a future," (Jeremiah 29:11 NIV).

The Bible says further in 2 Corinthians 1:20 NIV, *"For all the promises of God in Him are Yes, and in Him Amen to the glory of God through us."*

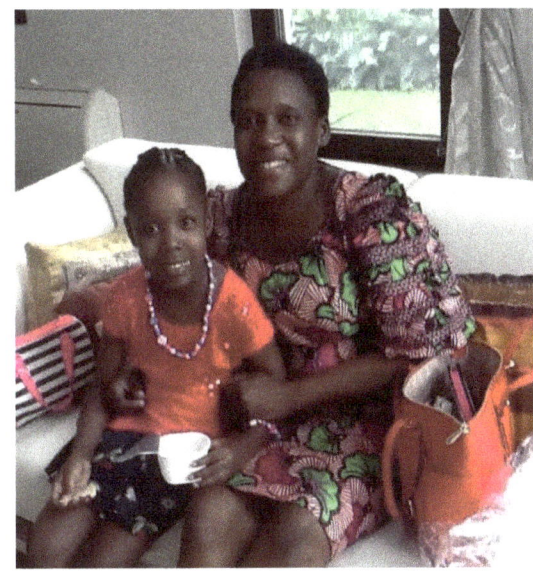 

Faith above with her promised child EWOBOLUWATITO which means, 'Look at how great and mighty God is!' EWO means 'see or look at.' Although Faith calls her by her full name, in school they call her EBT or TITO. EWO will be thirteen in July of 2022.

An Oasis in Malaysia

Photo by May, during Oasis Meeting

Malaysia was a dream that I had prayed for many years before seeing it come into fruition. Let me tell you about the goodness of the Lord!

While living in Nigeria, I met some wonderful Malaysian people. I determined in my heart that I wanted to put my foot on the soil of Asia because of their walk with the Lord. Of course, my husband dampened my spirit by jolting me back to reality and explaining all the reasons WHY we could never live in Malaysia. I looked at him, nodded my head but in my secret closet, continued to pray.

On one occasion when my husband's boss traveled to Malaysia for a meeting and so enthralled was he with the country, that he decided to move the entire team there for a year! In the mechanism of business, it did not make sense. But in the spiritual realm, my God had answered prayer!

Arriving in that beautiful country, I was numb with the knowledge of knowing we were really there. Malaysia is a Muslim country with three ethnicities: The Malay, The Chinese, and The Indians. The Malay ran the government, The Chinese the economy, and the Indians were considered lowest on the totem pole. Even within the Indian culture there was a system of castes that defined them as a people.

Yet I fell in love with this diverse group of people in one country. I wanted to benefit from my time being there. I whispered to my husband, "I hope we are still here for my 50th birthday. I'd like to invite my friends to celebrate with me in Malaysia."

Again, Clement scowled at me and simply said in his matter-of-fact way, "This assignment is for one year!"

We stayed for nearly seven! I invited some of my closest friends to celebrate both my husband's 50th birthday and a few years later, my own! God is SO good!

My ex-manager David Jackson (who shared his story of forgiveness) from my Congo days, happened to be living in Malaysia when we arrived. His wife and I were good friends. Jody left me a letter about the different schools to visit, neighborhoods to peruse for housing and a Bible Study to attend. I met the Bible Study leader, Susanne for lunch, and this is what she said, "I can leave Malaysia now because the Lord said you will be the next leader of this Bible Study." I was NOT about to take on this kind of leadership! I shook my head and retreated.

We visited the church David had recommended and met the Pastor and his wife Lisa Great (whose story is also included in this book). Getting to know them over time, I shared how this Ladies' Bible Study Leader wanted me to assume her responsibilities once she left. They persuaded me to do so and promised to be my covering. That is how I entered a Covenant with a group of women from diverse backgrounds, tongues, and creed.

Isaiah 49:22 NIV,

"See, I will beckon to the nations,
I will lift up my banner to the peoples;"

The banner which the Lord lifted was one of Salvation. The Lord told me when I was in my secret place praying, to call this ladies' group *'Oasis,'* for He would make it an Oasis in the desert of Malaysia for the expats (foreigners) who lived there.

Later while discussing with Susanne, she told me she had always felt the Bible Study to be an oasis in Kuala Lumpur. We grew from 13 members to over 50 ladies attending Bible Study at one time, under one roof! The Lord always provided a home to house and to nourish this group, both physically and spiritually!

Our selfless hostesses were a big part of the success and running of Oasis but so were the *Head of Small Groups* leader Barb Angell, our *Leading Ladies* (facilitators), and many others. Oasis continues to grow under the leadership of Loma Steynberg, to whom I did a proper handover before I left. Without realizing it, God developed our small group of ladies into an organization!

Today hundreds from different nations and tongues have sat at the feet of Jesus in an Oasis Meeting. We have become a network of women that sometimes find ourselves in the same country or city. We are a Sisterhood if you will. We have a special bond that has transcended and crossed race, language, and social status. I am privileged to have been a part of this work God has started and I know He is faithful to complete it!

Oasis Ladies throwing a baby shower for a member. We also celebrated birthdays, supported many causes in Malaysia as well as outside the country.

Above: Another Oasis Meeting, no matter how large we got, the Lord always provided the space we needed.

Elena's Re-story, Congo/Russia
My Testimony

Elena Moussounda – Oasis Member (kneeling on previous page, right side of the table, orange dress). Here she is with her husband Jean Alexis.

My husband and I met Elena when we went to our twins' school for a play, in which her child was also a part of the cast. When my husband saw the last name on the program, he told me that it was a Congolese name. I was pleasantly surprised because in all our years of expatriation, we had never worked in the same place as other Congolese. We made it a point to meet her and voila! She was partially Congolese and partially Russian AND to top it off, we knew some of the same people from Congo!

Of course, I invited her to an Oasis meeting and that was the beginning of a long relationship that continues until today, with me as her Spiritual Mom. Thozama had just left Kuala Lumpur and a spot was available in my *Upper Room – The Secret Place* and she earned it! There, I taught her the Word of God and how to pray. Her faith grew as she became hungrier for the things of God.

We enjoyed doing *Christmas Around the World Together* and I virtually introduced her to everyone I knew and brought her to our church. She accepted the Lord eagerly and was a formidable disciple! She brought her entire family, and they were converted and became active members of our congregation.

When her mother-in-law passed, she asked the church choir to come to her home to sing songs during the wake. Her personality, warmth and love were contagious!

After twelve years, we are both living again in the same city of Houston, which is almost as boisterous as Kuala Lumpur but not as densely populated and there are no Twin Towers here!
But we have found an extended family of former Oasis members and new ones. Elena and I continue to build onto the solid foundation we started in Kuala Lumpur. She is a part of a vibrant church where her family attends, and she is a regular participant of Bible Study and women retreats. Currently, she is helping in the Children's Ministry.

Elena's Re-story

Mama Rhonda has been my *Spiritual Mom* for almost 12 years now. She is a part of our family. I do not take any decisions before discussing with her and she leads me in prayer. She is attentive, caring and she always has time to listen. I truly thank God for having placed her on my path.

When I was going through a difficult patch, I visited her in Holland, and we had time to pray. It was like the old days in her *Upper Room - Secret Place*. When I lost my mother, she and her husband came to support us during the wake.

I cannot over-articulate the importance of having a *Spiritual Midwife* in one's life. My career as a professional midwife has taught me much in the natural sense, and I can see the same in the spiritual role Mama Rhonda plays in my life and the life of others.

For instance, the pain in a natural childbirth is the same as in a spiritual one. Birthing one's purpose and going through various issues in life can be extremely debilitating. The role of a midwife is to assist the mother to birth a child, the *Spiritual Midwife* does the same. She comes alongside her spiritual children and helps them birth their dreams. Helps them in life changing situations.

As a midwife, if we see the baby is in distress, we must provide additional help for the mother. It is the same with one's spiritual children. In addition to being a *Sage Femme* or midwife, you must have the capacity to love, to be patient and understanding.

One should be very blessed to have found a *Sage Femme* in one's life to help you navigate the storms and joys of living.

Rhonda and Elena. in Rhonda's home seated at her prayer bench

Treasury of Scripture – Words of Wisdom

Shiphrah and Puah – The Hebrew Midwives
Exodus 1:15-20

Shiphrah and Puah feared God and were blessed for it! The Bible says in Proverbs 9:10 NIV

"The fear of the LORD is the beginning of wisdom, and knowledge of the Holy One is understanding."

Let's see what these Midwives did to try to protect their Hebrew sons.

15 "The king of Egypt said to the Hebrew midwives, whose names were Shiphrah and Puah, 16 'When you are helping the Hebrew women during childbirth on the delivery stool, if you see that the baby is a boy, kill him; but if it is a girl, let her live.' 17 The midwives, however, feared God and did not do what the king of Egypt had told them to do; they let the boys live. 18 Then the king of Egypt summoned the midwives and asked them, 'Why have you done this? Why have you let the boys live?'
19 The midwives answered Pharaoh, 'Hebrew women are not like Egyptian women; they are vigorous and give birth before the midwives arrive.'
20 So God was kind to the midwives and the people increased and became even more numerous. 21 And because the midwives feared God, he gave them families of their own."

The Hebrew term translated '*the midwife*' (*hameyaledet*) may literally be translated '*the childbirth assisting woman.*' This term occurs in the singular (*midwife*) just three times: in Genesis 35:17, Genesis 38:28 and in Exodus 1:16.

The Hebrew term for *'birth stool'* in Exodus 1:16, *(obnayim)*, means literally *'two stones.'* It may refer to the primitive form of the birth-stool, which was simply two bricks (or stones) placed under each of the buttocks of the woman in labor.

We build our lives on the *'stone the builders rejected.'* It is this stone that makes our foundation secure. The Message Bible is clear.

*Jesus said, "Right—and you can read it for yourselves in your Bibles: The stone the masons threw out is now the cornerstone. This is God's work; we rub our eyes, we can hardly believe it! "This is the way it is with you. God's kingdom will be taken back from you and handed over to a people who will live out a kingdom life. Whoever stumbles on this Stone gets shattered; whoever the Stone falls on gets smashed," (*Matthew 21:42-43, The Message Bible).

I would rather you sat on those two stones to give birth to your project or your dreams, than to build on a faulty foundation. Build your life on Jesus and the Word of God. People rejected Jesus and His Word. John says he is THE WORD. When he spoke, crowds came from everywhere to hear his wisdom.

Sitting on these two stones in childbirth makes a person vulnerable and somewhat transparent. You're put in a precarious situation for the *Sage Femme* to examine you, nothing hidden. Having a *Spiritual Sage Femme* is the same. If you truly want to grow spiritually, you must be transparent, nothing hidden.

My aim is for every Spiritual child to be built on a foundation that stands. I walk with you very closely for a season so that you learn the things of God and perfect your craft or obtain your goal. Then I'm always there when you need me, but I expect you to also assist another person on the birthing stool.

"The rain came down, the streams rose, and the winds blew and beat against that house; yet it did not fall, because it had its foundation on the rock," (Matthew 7:25 NIV).

Personal Reflections

_____

_____

_____

_____

Amelie's Re-story, Gabon
My Testimony

On the left is a photo of Amelie at Double Portion Church, me, and First Lady – Sis Moss. The Baptismal pool is behind us. Right – Photo of Amelie after gifting Pastor Moss with a shirt from Gabon.

I met Rhonda in Gamba, Gabon, when I was working for the same company as her husband. It was the most appropriate time of my life, a time of challenges and storms in my marital life!

She invited me to her house prayer fellowship, taking place on Wednesday evenings. There was a group of Christian employees gathering there for Bible study and prayer.

Though I told Rhonda that I was Catholic, she responded that it did not matter, I was welcome in the prayer group, all people regardless of their convictions had a seat.

So, on Wednesday evenings I would go to the fellowship and really enjoyed my time there. Almost all prayer meetings ended with delicious pastries, drinks, or a meal!

Rhonda's simplicity, humility and love made me stay and increased my thirst for the knowledge of Jesus. I learnt how to read the Bible comprehensively and how to pray with the Word of God.

One thing that made me grow further in my faith was when I noticed that all newborn Christians in the fellowship were *'spiritually clever'*. In fact, they were fast to discover answers or seemed to have a special discernment or insight in the knowledge of God that I did not possess. They had something more than me, something I could not explain, but something that made me understand that they were *'peculiar'*!

So, I said to myself, *"I must get that thing, that thing I do not have!"* I later discovered that it was the Holy Spirit that I was lacking!

Rhonda has always been so attentive to my complaints. She would visit me early some mornings to pray, with comforting words.

An invitation to visit her home in Alabama took me to what I was longing for: the Water and Holy Spirit Baptism! She took me to her church in Northport, Alabama, Double Portion, where I met Pastor Moss and got baptized. My baptism was a very special one. Pastor Moss filled the pool for me alone on a Tuesday. Her twins joined me as they saw me in the water!
Wow, what a joyful day it was! I will never forget it!

I remember her daughter rehearsing for a play with this passage *"Jesus Christ is the same yesterday, and today and forever" (Hebrews 13:8 KJV)*. These words entered my heart for good!

Rhonda encouraged me to believe and always pray, she made me understand that God is never late, that only God can order the path of the righteous, that God cares for us.

Since then, I have stayed the course. I abide in the Word of Truth, with confidence and love.

Personal Reflections

_____

_____

_____

_____

_____

Treasury of Scripture – Words of Wisdom

The Art of Silence

One thing that I taught Amelie was the art of silence. This weapon she has learned to use skillfully and to keep securely in her arsenal.

There is a woman in the Bible who only has one or two references, yet her story is not only mysterious but powerful in that she did not speak.

In mentoring my spiritual children, I often teach them the *Art of Silence* especially in Matters of the Heart. I learned the hard way, so that is why I take extra special time to ensure that this craft is not only learned but correctly lived out in any situation when necessary.

This nameless woman is the Ethiopian married to Moses. She was his second wife, not Zipporah whom he had been married to for almost forty years. According to the Bible, he had recently married her and Miriam who had cared for her brother in the Nile River, watched over him and protected him, was no doubt unhappy about this union for reasons we can only imagine. The Ethiopian's story is tucked away in the pages of Numbers 12. She was undoubtedly a second wife taken by Moses and disliked by Aaron and Miriam. So much so that the Lord had to deal with Miriam by striking her with leprosy and putting her outside the camp!

Numbers 12:1-12 KJV,

¹"And Miriam and Aaron spake against Moses because of the Ethiopian woman whom he had married: for he had married an Ethiopian woman.

² And they said, 'Hath the Lord indeed spoken only by Moses? hath he not spoken also by us?' And the Lord heard it.
³ (Now the man Moses was very meek, above all the men which were upon the face of the earth.)
⁴ And the Lord spake suddenly unto Moses, and unto Aaron, and unto Miriam, 'Come out ye three unto the tabernacle of the congregation.' And they three came out.
⁵ And the Lord came down in the pillar of the cloud, and stood in the door of the tabernacle, and called Aaron and Miriam: and they both came forth.
⁶ And he said, 'Hear now my words: If there be a prophet among you, I the Lord will make myself known unto him in a vision and will speak unto him in a dream.
⁷ My servant Moses is not so, who is faithful in all mine house.
⁸ With him will I speak mouth to mouth, even apparently, and not in dark speeches; and the similitude of the Lord shall he behold: wherefore then were ye not afraid to speak against my servant Moses?'
⁹ And the anger of the Lord was kindled against them; and he departed.
¹⁰ And the cloud departed from off the tabernacle; and behold, Miriam became leprous, white as snow: and Aaron looked upon Miriam, and behold, she was leprous.
¹¹ And Aaron said unto Moses, 'Alas, my lord, I beseech thee, lay not the sin upon us, wherein we have done foolishly, and wherein we have sinned.
¹² Let her not be as one dead, of whom the flesh is half consumed when he cometh out of his mother's womb.'
¹³ And Moses cried unto the Lord, saying, 'Heal her now, O God, I beseech thee.'
¹⁴ And the Lord said unto Moses, 'If her father had but spit in her face, should she not be ashamed seven days? let her be shut out from the camp seven days, and after that let her be received in again.'"

Most of the time, women's names are not mentioned, words are not put in their mouths, or they are not allowed to say a word, and their achievements are behind the scenes in the Bible narratives. Passages that mention the presence and contribution of African women in the Bible are especially neglected; perhaps because there are few African women in the narratives.

The fact is that even though the Cushite woman was silent, her silence was meant to communicate something. To know what her silence means and communicates, it is important to understand how silence conveys a message. In other words, one must be familiar with silence as a cultural element, as well as the conversational functions and value of silence. In the light of the above semiotic meaning of silence in the African context, it suggests that the meaning of the *Ethiopian's* silence can possibly mean the following:

The African woman might have employed silence because she believed that God would fight for her and vindicate her; for an African woman in a polygamous house (who is a Christian Believer) whenever there was unbearable jealousy or strife beyond what she could handle, would say, *"I'm going to stand still and see the salvation of the Lord"* (Exodus 14:13-12 NIV). Or she might sing as Jehoshaphat ordered the singers to go forth singing in battle instead of taking carnal weapons they used singing as a weapon and won the battle (2 Chronicles 20:21-22 NIV)!

21 "After consulting the people, Jehoshaphat appointed men to sing to the Lord and to praise him for the splendor of his[c] holiness as they went out at the head of the army, saying:
'Give thanks to the Lord,
  for his love endures forever.'
22 As they began to sing and praise, the Lord set ambushes against the men of Ammon and Moab and Mount Seir who were invading Judah, and they were defeated."

On many occasions, I have used singing and praise when I felt that my prayers were weak, my praise was strong to the Creator of the Universe, The I AM that I AM!

In the book of Job, we see that the Lord was silent for over 37 chapters before He spoke! And even when God spoke, he didn't really address Job's complaints or his friends play of '*wisdom*,' rather God spoke of His splendor and grandiose power. He told of how He alone was the GREAT I AM. What a statement that was!

In Job's anguish, pain, and suffering, he had no doubt had lots of time to contemplate his fate and to ponder about God. In Psalm 46:10 NIV, the psalmist *says, "Be still, and know that I am God; I will be exalted among the nations, I will be exalted in the earth."* God is All powerful. This is a direct command from God to be quiet, lay down our weapons of warfare. Get rid of the senseless chatter and to be still in the presence of Almighty God. Job had learned in his distress the precious lesson of being silent and to be still and KNOW that "*I AM is God.*" The word to '*know*' in KJV was the same Hebrew word used in Genesis, "*Adam knew his wife and she conceived*" (Genesis 4:1). Therefore, *to know God alludes to a connotation of cultivating a deeper, more intimate relationship with Him.* Isaiah 55:9 says, "*God's ways are higher than our ways.*"

Then in Job 40:2 NLT, the Lord said to Job, "*Do you still want to argue with the Almighty? You are God's critic, but do you have the answers?*" Fortunately, earlier on in Job 28, he had recognized the wisdom of God in an interlude entitled, 'Where Wisdom is Found'. Though many commentaries argue Job could not have written such a beautiful poem, it suffices to say, someone did and why not Job? And it reads,

12But where can wisdom be found?
  Where does understanding dwell?
13 No mortal comprehends its worth;
  it cannot be found in the land of the living.

¹⁴ The deep says, "It is not in me";
  the sea says, "It is not with me."
¹⁵ It cannot be bought with the finest gold,
  nor can its price be weighed out in silver.

One commentary (Smick) argues, "The point is that man's intelligence and determination enable him to accomplish amazing feats of technological ingenuity but left to himself he cannot find wisdom. Wisdom is a treasure rarer than any other."

²⁰ Where then does wisdom come from?
  Where does understanding dwell?
²¹ It is hidden from the eyes of every living thing,
  concealed even from the birds in the sky.
²² Destruction and Death say,
  "Only a rumor of it has reached our ears."
²³ God understands the way to it
  and he alone knows where it dwells,
²⁴ for he views the ends of the earth
  and sees everything under the heavens.
²⁵ When he established the force of the wind
  and measured out the waters,
²⁶ when he made a decree for the rain
  and a path for the thunderstorm,
²⁷ then he looked at wisdom and appraised it;
  he confirmed it and tested it.
²⁸ And he said to the human race,
  "The fear of the Lord—that is wisdom,
  and to shun evil is understanding."

Job concluded this magnificent *discourse* by coming back to the touchstone of revelation. Undoubtedly, true and infinite wisdom is derived only from God. We discover it as Job did, by sitting at the feet of Jesus, reading, dissecting, and memorizing passages of scripture. By living right and having the *fear* of God. Job recited what is written in Proverbs 9:10 ESV, "*The fear of God is the beginning of wisdom, and the knowledge of the Holy One is insight.*" Proverbs, ladies, is an excellent "GO TO" for *wisdom scriptures*.

Interesting enough, the first woman Eve saw that the tree was pleasant to the eyes, and *a tree to be desired to make one wise*, they took and did eat (Genesis 3:6). Yet instead of becoming wiser, they lost all their wisdom becoming fools instead! This shall not be our portion in Jesus Name! May we be like Job, yielding our wills to the Master allowing him to write our *Re-Story*. The Message Bible says it beautifully in Psalm 18:24b, *"God rewrote the text of my life when I opened the book of my heart to his eyes."*
<u>Just Selah right there.</u>

I have learned much about *'The Art of Silence'* in various African Cultures. One thing our Congolese Pastor who was also a cardiologist, Dr Jeremy Kinouani said in a sermon referring to what *NOT* to do at a funeral, especially since it was a tragic one caused by the war in Congo. He said, *"One should not talk nonsense to fill in the silence during the wake, but one's words must be measured and wise, or it would be best to remain in silence."*

Following are Scriptures from the Bible (NIV) that speak about the **'Art of Silence'**. You would be wise to learn these verses as practicing the **'Art of Silence'** is easier said than done.

1. Ecclesiastes 9:17 NIV, *"The quiet words of the wise are more to be heeded than the shouts of a ruler of fools."*
2. Ecclesiastes 3:7-8 NIV, *"... a time to tear and a time to sew; a time to be silent and a time to speak; a time to love and a time to hate; a time for war and a time for peace.*
3. Proverbs 17:28 NIV, *"Even fools are thought wise when they keep silent, with their mouths shut, they seem intelligent."*
4. Proverbs 10:19 NIV, *"Transgression is a work where people talk too much, but anyone who holds his tongue is prudent."*
5. Proverbs 21:23 NIV, *"Whoever guards his mouth, and his tongue keeps himself out of trouble."*
6. Psalm 141:3 NIV, *"O Lord, set a guard at my mouth, Keep watch over the door of my lips."*
7. Psalm 62:5-6 NIV, *"My soul, wait in silence for God only, for my hope is from Him. He only is my rock and my salvation, my stronghold; I shall not be shaken."*

I believe the Ethiopian was silent because she knew she had done no wrong and the Lord would fight her battle. From the reading, we see God did just that! He silenced Miriam by putting her outside of the camp, striking her with leprosy!

Therefore, the next time you get into a fiery argument with your spouse, colleague, or someone else, keep quiet. Not only will it bring an uncomfortable silence which brings on *peace in your spirit*, but the Lord shows up to vindicate you!

Psalm 37:7 NIV --*"Be silent in the LORD's presence and wait patiently for him. Don't be angry because of the one whose way prospers or the one who implements evil schemes."*

Getting rid of the Yokes

"Trust in the Lord with all your heart and lean not on your own understanding. Acknowledge him in all your ways and he will direct your path," Proverbs 3:5 NIV.

Jesus was a skilled carpenter, having had Joseph, his earthly father, teach him the tricks of the trade. He knew something about yokes that went on oxen. Every yoke was different. To receive anything from the Lord we must first come to Him and have faith and we must believe He is the rewarder of those who diligently seek Him.

In Easton's Bible Dictionary, a yoke is defined to be: Fitted on the neck of oxen for the purpose of binding to them the traces by which they might draw the plow. (Numbers 19:2, Deuteronomy 21:3).
It was a curved piece of wood called 'ol. Essentially, a yoke was a harness used by oxen and other animals to ease the work of hauling a load. It was also meant as a designation of servitude and carrying the burden of a task or mission.

When Jesus said, *"Take my yoke upon you"* (Matthew 11:29), He meant that we are to submit ourselves to Him every day in every way. A yoke was made of wood, hand carved to fit the neck and shoulders of the animal to prevent pain or discomfort. In ancient culture, the word 'yoke' was a term that was used to describe submission. So, when someone was described as being yoked to someone or something, it was communicating the idea that he or she was in submission to that person or thing.

So, to be yoked to Jesus is to serve and obey Him. Before you bristle at that idea, consider this: everyone is yoked to someone or something. The question is, to whom or what do you want to be yoked? Some are yoked to the power of sin. They are under its control. Some are yoked in a relationship with unbelievers, and the Bible warns very specifically against that (see 2 Corinthians 6:14).

Years ago, while living in Pointe Noire in Congo, I enjoyed a life of fasting and prayer. During one of these times, I was at the office and saw a colleague who thanked me profusely for the help my husband had provided for her. She went on to extol her gratitude, why, not only had he been gracious enough to help her move but used our vehicle to do so!

At the very same time, I had to rent a truck and organize all the moving from one house to a newer one and had used a friend to assist me. Holy anger rose in me that I could not control! The old spirit of jealousy overtook me! I stormed to my husband's office threatening to splash coffee on him, rightfully so, wouldn't you think? But God did not! The Holy Spirit ordered me to leave the building and return home, which I did expediently. Arriving home, the Lord commanded me to go to my private place of prayer and drop to the floor in a posture of servitude, lying prostrate on the hard stone floor. As I cried out to God, he silenced me and commanded me to turn to the following Scripture.

Yoke and Discipleship

Isaiah 58: 3-6 NIV

³ "'Why have we fasted,' they say,
  'and you have not seen it?
Why have we humbled ourselves,
  and you have not noticed?'
Yet on the day of your fasting, you do as you please
  and exploit all your workers.
⁴ Your fasting ends in quarreling and strife,
  and in striking each other with wicked fists.
⁵You cannot fast as you do today
  and expect your voice to be heard on high."
⁶Is not this the kind of fasting I have chosen: to loosen the chains of injustice and untie the cords of the yoke, to set the oppressed free and break every yoke?'"

The Lord showed me how my day of fasting ended with quarreling and strife, and this should not be so for a woman of God. The Lord reminded me how silence would have been the best policy in this regard. How I could have waited till both my husband, and I were home in the evening, and I could have quietly questioned him about this situation explaining my displeasure and why. Instead, in the heat of the moment, I almost caused a scene!

My husband's name is Clement (meaning *kind and generous*), he would help ANYONE in need (even to his demise) and I knew that. He was an accountant at the time and worked long hours and had given me the necessary funds to implement the house move. I secretly resented that he was not always available to help. His job also caused him to travel a lot and many times the children and I accompanied him. The thing the Lord wanted me to do most of all, was get rid of my unfounded jealousy that I was yoked to. Jesus, if we're willing, releases the yoke of our oppression and encourages us to take on *His yoke* instead.

You see, Jesus was teaching me way back then to abandon my ways for His. The Bible declares in Isaiah 55 that His ways are higher than our ways. I had to completely submit myself to the Father to become the *'Sage Femme'* -- the Midwife he had ordained me to be from the foundations of the earth! It involves relinquishing my will for God's. Now that's a high and lofty statement!

Therefore, consider the context of Jesus' words. Two oxen are chosen to share a yoke. The first is an older seasoned ox. He is trained and hardy from years of routine. The second is a new young ox. He has potential but is inexperienced. By sharing the same yoke with a veteran workhorse, the elder trains the young.

Not only that, but the experienced one draws harder, to bear the majority of the load. Since the older one leads, the younger ox does not have to wonder what to do. He learns from his mentor and gains the knowledge and skill to teach others.

Such a powerful revelation that I had to learn in my twenties in a distant land where I chose to be yoked to the Father.

The Lord had me return to that young girl in the office and disciple her. When she was without shelter and job, I brought her into my home and helped her. This is what it means to disciple others.

I have learned to mentor others through my own personal experiences. I have a heart for people and a passion to assist them at their point of need. I have carried willingly the burdens of others and gone beyond the call of my duty and my comfort, to ensure that they feel safe and loved. I have tried to exhibit the love of Christ as this passage of Scripture admonishes us to do in Colossians 1:27-28, (The Voice Translation):

27 "He decided to make known to them His blessing to the nations; the glorious riches of this mystery is the indwelling of the Anointed in you! The very hope of glory.
28 We are preaching Him—spreading the Word to all with equal amounts of wise warning and instruction—so that, at the final judgment, we will be able to present everyone to the Creator fully mature because of what Jesus the Anointed, our Liberating King, has done.
29 Therefore, I continue to toil and struggle—because his amazing power and energy surge within me."

Thozama's Re-story, South Africa
My Testimony

I was in 2012, when my family moved to Malaysia that I met my dear friend Rhonda, the leader of Oasis Bible Study Group. We clicked the first day we met.

I became part of the prayer team. There was a prayer basket where members put in their prayer requests. From this basket, I compiled a list of the prayer items. Rhonda made me pray for these prayer requests in front of everyone every Thursday. That was nerve-wrecking for me. In my life, I had never prayed in public. As far as I was concerned, I did not know how to, but guess what, there is a first time for everything!

One day, we decided that we would meet once a week at her house. It was in her study room, which we fondly called the 'upper room' that these powerful prayer sessions were held. We prayed for each prayer request. Some of the people we had never met before. It was so fulfilling to hear updates of answered prayers. The outcome was not always what we prayed for, but as painful as it was, we trusted and obeyed. At the time I was going through a difficult time with my son. He had developmental delays, mainly speech delay, amongst others. Back at home, after several speech therapy sessions, from the age of 18 months he did not respond at all. At the age of 4, he was not talking. I consulted quite a few specialist doctors.

There was one doctor who diagnosed him with autism. I remember telling the doctor that as the mother of the child, I did not agree with that diagnosis. Here I am narrating my encounter with the doctor to Rhonda. Her response was straightforward, "Never label your child." Thank you to the Oasis team, my son is now healthy and strong,
doing very well at school.

A few years later, I told Rhonda about my depression, the suicidal thoughts and that I had just come out of hospital. The only thing that kept me from entertaining the suicidal thoughts was my mother and my beautiful children. When I remember how my mother felt when we lost our sister in 1984, I just could not let her go through that pain again. Also, I could not bear the thought of my children growing up without me. I would have failed them, so I had to fight.

All that she said was, "Oh! child of God I need to wean you off of that medication, you need to come out of that depression." I did not say anything, but I knew deep down that what she was saying was impossible, because I had multiple relapses and my doctor had mentioned to me that now it might be a permanent illness, and if at all, it would take me an exceedingly long time to be on remission again. I was put on chronic medication with five different types of tablets. I gained weight, low self-esteem, doing my motherly responsibilities was a mission. I could not pray anymore and so on. I felt the emptiness, loneliness, and the anguish. Life was terrible. Again, I phoned her, we prayed and prayed and prayed. To cut the story short, I have been off the medication for two years now.

For several years, there had been something that had been bothering me, but I could not get to the bottom of it. There had always been a deep-seated feeling that there was something awry about my life. It is this mystery that led to my depressive episodes. I had reached a point where I refused to allow something unknown to me, to control my life so that is how I managed to be on remission. I will not lie and say it did not bother me anymore, but it was not going to control my life.

Just when I thought the worst was over, one day, I was just sitting at home minding my own business, when I got a gentle nudge to do something, and I ignored it. It then became an instruction. The first day I obeyed, oh boy, I was dumbfounded! Finally, I had a revelation, the naked truth about what had been going on around me. As I was still battling with this truth in my mind not knowing what to do, it was lockdown due to the Corona Virus pandemic.

It happened so fast. There is some truth in this proverb, "Every cloud has a silver lining." If it was not for the lockdown, life would have swallowed me, I am telling you the honest truth. It gave me time to reflect, gather my thoughts on how to tackle the situation at my own pace without the usual hustle and bustle.

During this difficult time, there was only one person I could think of and that was Rhonda. She is always just a phone call away. Through her prayers and wise counsel, here I am today still standing. What I learnt out of all this; you must know your battles. You can never fight a spiritual battle in the natural. When you surrender all to Abba the Father, the Mighty Warrior, the only one who is great in battle, he will fight your battles. Your duty is to be still. In 1 Samuel 17:45 NIV, *"But David said to the Philistine, 'You come against me with sword and spear and javelin, but I come against you in the name of the LORD of Hosts'."*

One more thing, forgive every day, manage your thoughts and emotions, do not make assumptions, and avoid being angry. That inner peace is important. Thank you, Rhonda, for your wise counsel.

There are several lessons I have learnt from Rhonda.

1. Confess your sins.
2. Power of prayer and pray every day.
3. Faith and power of a positive mind
4. Intentional use of words e.g. Don't say *'if God helps me'* instead say *'when God helps me'* because he will.
5. True meaning and the power of forgiveness.
6. Giving and tithing.

In conclusion, there is truth in the Scripture that says, *"God will never leave you nor forsake you."* 1 Corinthians 10:13 NIV, *"The temptations in your life are no different from what others experience. And God is faithful. He will not allow the temptation to be more than you can stand. When you are tempted, He will show you a way out so that you can endure."*

When I reflect, for each encounter that I had in my life, God has always been there with me, there was not a single moment that I was alone even though I may not have been aware at the time. My last encounter excites me the most because he prepared me beforehand so that I could endure.

Imagine a situation where I was still depressed, weak and confused. All of that had to get out of the way. Thank you, Abba, for your love, for your care, for your guidance and for your wisdom. When I go astray, as my Shepherd you always guide me, and it does not end there, you lead the way. As I am writing this, I feel a sense of guilt because I am not doing enough for God. I don't know what makes me deserve all this grace.

Thank you, Rhonda, for being obedient and allowing God to use you. I will always treasure the day I met you. Some of the Scriptures that came through to mind as I was writing:

Isaiah 48:17 NIV -- *"Thus says the LORD your Redeemer, the Holy One of Israel: 'I am the LORD your God, who teaches you for your benefit, who directs you in the way you should go'."*

Psalm 32:8 NIV -- *"I will instruct you and teach you the way you should go; I will give you counsel and watch over you."*

Isaiah 30:2 NIV -- *"And whether you turn to the right or to the left, your ears will hear this command behind you: 'This is the way. Walk in it'."*

Psalm 23:1 NIV -- *"The LORD is my shepherd; I shall not be in want. He restores my soul. He guides me in paths of righteousness for his name's sake. Even though I walk through the valley of the shadow of death, I will fear no evil, for you are with me; your rod and your staff, they comfort me."*

Psalm 86 and Psalm 91 are two other passages of Scripture that have served me well over these last few years!

Treasury of Scripture – Words of Wisdom

God Delivers us from Depression and Suicide

The Bible says in Psalm 107:20 BSB -- *"He sent forth His word and healed them; He rescued them from the Pit."* Sometimes depression makes you feel like you are in a pit! The enemy delights to keep you there and indeed to bury you! He is doing his job. *"The thief's purpose is to steal and kill and destroy. My purpose is to give them a rich and satisfying life"* (John 10:10 NLT).

Please notice in the case of Thozama how often she recited the Word of God. Also, remember that she DID not know how to pray, prior to coming to KL and being trained during our sessions together. The elements of The Word of God and Prayer CANNOT be separated. I always like to ask people when they send me a prayer request, to give me the Scripture that they are standing on. This helps them to learn to pray Scripture and to employ that Word correctly in their lives. This is the case of Thozama.

When depression, anxiety and suicidal thoughts plague you, do not feel guilty if you need to get professional medical help but also use the Word of God as your weapon!

Speak to your SOUL, which is the seat of your emotions. Pray this Scripture over yourself and then BELIEVE what you have spoken. Believe the Words of the Lord for your life. I've used the New International Version for the sake of clarity but feel free to read this version from The Passion Bible or even King James Version. The Word never loses its power!

Psalm 103, NIV

¹ "Praise the Lord, my soul;
　all my inmost being, praise his holy name.
² Praise the Lord, my soul,
　and forget not all his benefits—
³ who forgives all your sins
　and heals all your diseases,
⁴ who redeems your life from the pit
　and crowns you with love and compassion,
⁵ who satisfies your desires with good things
　so that your youth is renewed like the eagle's.

Nathalie's Re-story, Lebanon
My Testimony

I remember meeting Nathalie in the gym. She was so inquisitive, everything I told her about that was spiritual, she had a rebuttal! She clearly thought about everything in the natural sense till I introduced her to Jesus Christ, and she made Him her Lord and Savior. Nathalie began to get to know God and trust Him with her very life.

My husband and I had difficulties having children and the only way we could conceive was through IVF. So, we took that route and what a difficult, stressful, and expensive route it was to take!

For my first child, I did 7 or maybe 8 IVF cycles. We had done so many cycles that I lost track of their exact number. In my case, each cycle was a fresh cycle because I was a poor responder to IVF medication, which meant that I could not produce enough good quality eggs to freeze for potential subsequent cycles.

At every attempt, I had to re-start the process from its very beginning. This increased the length and cost of every cycle and of course the stress levels. After a couple of years trying and several failed attempts, we had our first child, a girl. I was 35 years old at the time. We were beyond happy. I never thought I was ever going to have a child of my own.

My daughter was born in Kuala Lumpur, Malaysia where I met Rhonda. Not too long after my daughter was born, I started desiring a second child. Remembering the pain, despair, hopelessness, the money, and time we spent trying for our first child, I thought this would be out of the question for us. On top of that, my husband, too, must undergo an uncomfortable procedure when we do IVF.

Despite of it all, I could not stop thinking of trying for another child. Finally, after almost 2 years of longing for a second child, I mustered up my courage, and shared my desire and thoughts with my husband. To my surprise he welcomed the idea. Part of me was feeling excited but another part was scared and worried. Nevertheless, we started trying for a second child.

Fast forward and here I am at the egg retrieval stage of my IVF treatment. I remember the day I was going for the procedure as if it were yesterday. It was dawn, somewhere between 5:00 and 6:00 am. I was getting into my car to go to the clinic for my procedure. I saw a woman, during her morning walk, pass across in front of my car as I was pulling out of my driveway. For some strange unexplainable reason, I felt drawn to her. I felt I needed to talk to her. I felt she could help me, guide me, and support me with what I was going through. I so wished I could just simply walk up to her and tell her where I was going, and what I was going to do and ask her to help me and to be by my side. This woman was Rhonda. Again, this IVF attempt was unsuccessful! We almost gave up trying, but my husband and I decided on one more last cycle, after which if we were unsuccessful, we would stop and put the dream of having a second child behind us.

A few weeks later I saw Rhonda again in the gym in the compound where we both lived. It was there the first time I spoke to her. After that we started noticing each other around the compound and chatted to each other. In no time we became friends and morning walk buddies. During our walks we spoke about almost everything; our families, plans for the day, experiences, work, food, faith, and God.

During one of our walks, I opened up to her about my fertility struggles. Rhonda's response simply came as... *"Ah not to worry. You have come to the right place. That is what I do. That is my specialty. I pray for women seeking to have children. God has made me a spiritual 'Sage Femme'/ midwife to bring children into their purpose."* Next, she took me to her house into her study room and showed me pictures of several people she had prayed for to have children. While standing there admiring these pictures and thinking how much I wanted my picture to be among them, Rhonda told me with no hesitation, that the next picture was going to be of me and my new baby.

What happened next was a journey of faith in God, which Rhonda took me on holding my hand at every step of the way. She stood by me, supported me, cheered me on and prayed for me at every twist and turn of my new journey of faith and conception.

My first step was to find a new fertility doctor for my second and final attempt. I was given the name of a doctor who I was told was good but, on the flipside was way too pricey. Deep down I thought this will be nothing but another useless and waste of money exercise. I decided I would go to see him anyway. Rhonda prayed with me the day before my appointment, asking God to help me make the right decision and went to the appointment with me. When we came out Rhonda encouraged me to go ahead with this doctor. To Rhonda, the doctor sounded good enough, but it is God who I need to trust and rely on, that my treatment and eventual success was in God's hands, not the doctor's. The doctor is a tool that God will use to fulfil my purpose.

I started my last and final IVF but this time I was equipped with essential tools that I did not have in all my previous trials: prayer and belief in the power and grace of God.

From the start of the process till its end, Rhonda prayed for me. She prayed for me in faith and in joy; in faith because God had listened and delivered and in joy because I had already received.

I am so grateful that God has put Rhonda on my path. She opened my eyes to how powerful and strong I am as an individual. She made me realize that feelings of despair and helplessness, negative thoughts and doubt in my ability to conceive will only shut my spirit and body down and prevent me from achieving my purpose of having a child. God wants happiness and greatness for us and wants us to achieve our purpose.

Nine months later at the age of 38, I had my second child, a baby girl Isla. To me she is a miracle from God.

Rhonda had one more unfinished task to complete. When she came to see my newborn for the first time, she held her in her arms and lifted her up to the sky and said a little prayer, a prayer of praise and thanks to the Lord for His goodness and kindness. To me this act not only honored and glorified the Lord but also showered my daughter with His eternal blessings and entrusted her into His safe protective hands.

*"Rhonda, honestly, I genuinely believe that if it were not for you, I wouldn't have had Isla. You are my spiritual Godmother as you were the only person in my life who properly introduced me to faith, God and helped me understand gratefulness to God and having a life of joy and abundance that God has given me. When you lifted Isla up to God, that was an act of baptism. I probably never told you that but, in my heart, you are her true Godmother. Isla is a true miracle of God. This has made me understand better how to live a life of gratefulness to God **for the life** of joy and abundance He has given me."*

Rhonda and Isla

Chelsa's Re-story, USA
My Testimony

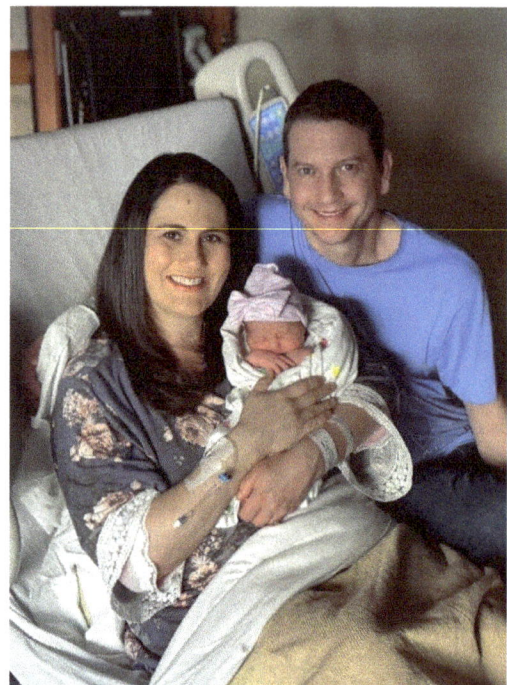
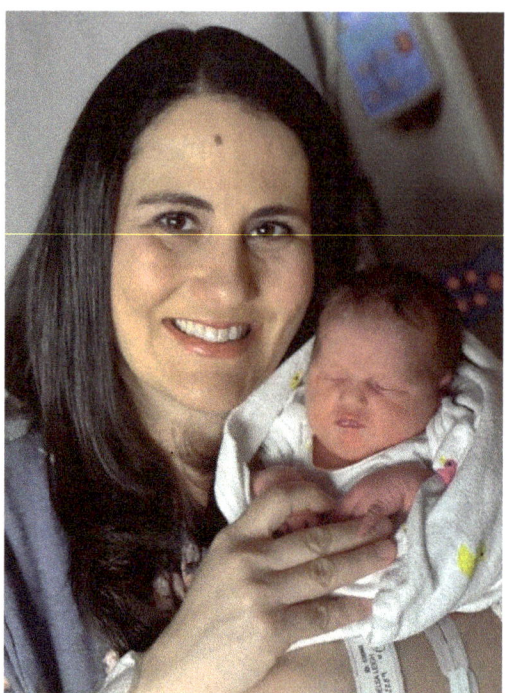

The happy couple after miraculous birth of baby Sarah!

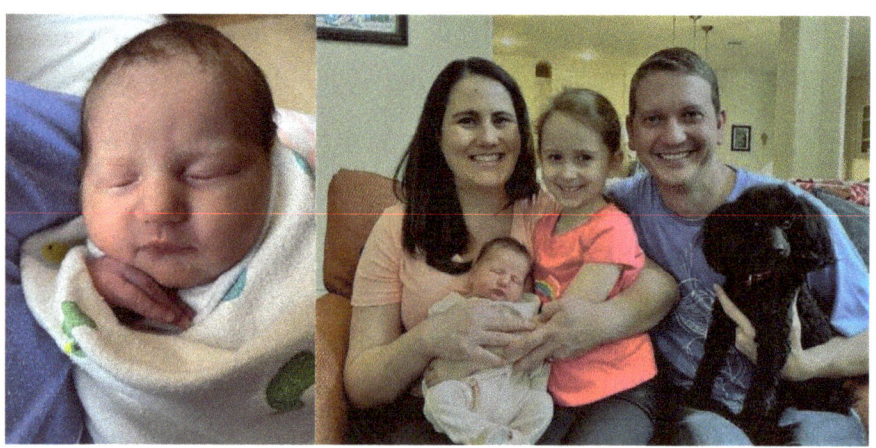

Child of the Promise with her big sister.

"He gives the barren woman a home, making her the joyous mother of children. Praise the LORD!" (Psalm 113:9 NIV).

I first met Chelsa at a women's luncheon. She told of her infertility issues, and I invited her to attend my **Release the Dove Bible Study**, which she did. At the onset of the study, the Lord began to do miraculous things in her marriage and in her home. Her husband went from being home and depressed, to getting saved and baptized! Hallelujah!

Together, they were able to believe God for a child. At the end of the study, I prayed for every woman who attended by placing my Jerusalem prayer shawl over them, declaring the Word God released for each individual and their situation. For Chelsa, I told her two things. I put my prayer shawl around her waist and commanded her to be fertile. I told her she would have a baby soon. I also told her that in 2020, she would be working from home. Chelsa marveled at both revelations, remembering how the failed IVF treatment had dampened their faith, and there would be no way that she could work from home.

The Holy Spirit knew that COVID would hit and that she *would* work from home! Below is an excerpt from her praise report!

"Hello friends! Surprise!! We are so very excited to announce the arrival of our baby girl, Sarah Liana! She is a true miracle, and an answer to our prayers—the child of God's promise."

Born on 3/11/2021 at 10:59 pm
6 lbs. 5 oz and 19 inches long

After experiencing the brokenness brought by devastating losses, a failed IVF cycle, and being told the odds were against us, we submitted to the apparent reality that our window of opportunity had passed. We then experienced the true healing, peace, and freedom that only God can provide — surrendering everything to Him and living in the overflowing abundance of His love and blessings. Then out of nowhere, the most unexpected thing happened in the midst of this most difficult COVID season. God surprised us with a baby girl we never imagined we'd receive. He decided to bless us exceedingly and abundantly more than we could ever ask or imagine. Proving He is sovereign over everything, He can and will overcome the most impossible odds, He is SO good and faithful, and His ways are so much better than our ways!

It is our prayer that our story encourages any of you who are lost and hurting, or perhaps struggling with loss and infertility the way we did. May you look upon Sarah and see the abundance of His unfailing love and unsurpassable power. May our family serve the Lord always and bring honor and glory to His name!"

God did two other remarkable things for Chelsa and Ryan that blew their minds! He gave Chelsa a new and better job still working from home! Chelsa came unexpectedly to our zoom prayer group one day just when I was testifying on how we had been able to sell our home after years of inability to do so. Chelsa chimed in with her prayer request stating they also had rental property they had been trying to sell for years and wanted God to open the door for them to do so. I used the sale of our house as a point of contact and reference commanding that their house sale would occur in much less time than ours. God brought that miracle to pass in record time!!! **God definitely is THE God of the exceedingly abundantly more than you can ever dream, imagine or ask!!!**

Kirsten's Re-story, Italy
My Testimony

I met Rhonda through a friend of mine here in Italy. It was in May 2020 when I was invited to attend an online women's conference call. This was during the lockdown in Italy, as well as in the USA.

I had been speaking to God about having a mentor in my life over the last few weeks before this event. I recall having this strong urge to have a spiritual mentor and wondering who I could ask to walk my spiritual journey with me.

When my friend invited me to this conference, I had been working from home and knew I would not be able to attend the full conference but was hoping to at least attend some part of it.

Thank God I was able to attend just at the right time. I remember so clearly that there was the discussion about The Lord's Prayer. I remembered thinking, how simple, The Lord has told us exactly what to pray for, because He knew exactly what our needs would be. I also remember hearing Rhonda speaking, and her voice was so powerful and so soothing, like a mother's touch. At that very moment I knew she was the answer to the prayer I had.

I immediately wrote my friend and asked her to put me in contact with Rhonda. A week later I reached out to Rhonda, and we had set up our first call.
We spoke and I felt that I had known Rhonda for years – everything felt so easy and so smooth. I confided in Rhonda and felt I had a safe place.

I told Rhonda that I longed to speak in tongues, that I had many soul-ties I needed to break, that I longed for marriage and having kids, and that I wanted to know God's purpose for my life.

I can tell you that I had prayed for many years about receiving the gift of speaking in tongues. I prayed for so long, and I was at a stage where I felt it would never happen. During our call we also discussed whether I had been baptized by the Holy Spirit (I at that stage, did not understand what this meant, as I had been baptized in water, but could not understand why this was different).

We then planned to set up another call a few weeks later, where Rhonda had sent me some homework, prayers, and fasting that I needed to prepare before the call.

The day of our call, I can only tell you that God spoke to me. During the fasting, and during the praying, I felt God release me from chains, I felt Him show me His promises. Each prayer Rhonda sent me, was specifically meant for me. Wow. I was in awe – God had used these prayers to release me and set me free.

I remember starting the call with Rhonda - I told her my visions that I had been having and the chains that I felt God was releasing me from. We then prayed and I remember speaking about the gift of speaking in tongues, Rhonda asking me to start releasing what was in my heart, and when it came out, wow at first, I could not understand what it was, then there was this warm burning sensation in my stomach, moving to my chest and I could not stop. I was receiving the Baptism of the Holy Spirit and being released with the gift of speaking in tongues.

All these years I prayed; God sent me a Spiritual Mother who helped me to release what God had inside of me.

This was the beginning of my and Rhonda's relationship as mother and daughter in Christ. Our journey has been nothing but blessed – I have not met Rhonda in life, we have had a virtual relationship – but I feel that I have known Rhonda all my life. She was sent from God into my life. We have realized how many things we have in common, and how amazing it is to know that God knew at the exact time, the exact person to send into my life.

He planned it perfectly, He ordained it at the right moment. He sent my friend into my life, who would then allow me to come to meet Rhonda. God is powerful and almighty, He is still working in my life, and although I am yet to see the harvest that He has in store for me and all His promises come to pass, however I can tell you that He gave me the desire to want a mentor, and He delivered on this desire. He did not only send me someone who was a random choice, but He carefully selected her because we had walked some similar paths, and He knew exactly when and how I would need this mentor.

After years of praying for the blessing of speaking in tongues and after a long time of praying and desiring a mentor, God has opened it all for me. God is awesome! His promises never return void. He gives us the dreams and desires in our hearts because He wants to lead us to the destiny that He has in store for us, and to bring us a little closer to Heaven each time.

Thank you.
Kirsten, Italy

Viki's Re-story,
My Testimony

I am grateful God put Rhonda in my life when I was living in the Netherlands, working as a nanny. We went to the same church, and she invited me to be part of the Bible Study Group she was hosting at her place. We were studying a book called, "Too Busy Not to Pray", which totally transformed my prayer life.

Rhonda was the first person I was able to open to about a struggle I had been fighting for years. Her first reaction was to fast and pray with me. She would often counsel me and mentor me personally too. She really inspired me to lead worship and grow in this gift God gave me. Once she prophesied over me and told me God does not want my songs to only stay in my notebooks, they needed to be heard.

Not only did Rhonda have a spiritual impact on my life but she also inspired me in a practical sense. I would watch her host people and welcome them lovingly in her home. I desired to imitate that.

I had a dream to go to Australia and do a discipleship training, but I needed money for that. Rhonda got a few other ladies from church involved in a fundraiser event for me. I am grateful for all she has poured into my life. I am reaping daily the benefits of all I learned from her.

Daria's Re-story, USA
My Testimony

The writer of Hebrews instructs us in chapter 13 verses 7 and 17 respectively to "Remember your leaders, who spoke the Word of God to you. Consider the outcome of their way of life and imitate their faith" and to "Have confidence in your leaders and submit to their authority, because they keep watch over you as those who must give an account. Do this so that their work will be a joy, not a burden, for that would be of no benefit to you". I could stop right here because this describes what Rhonda has been to me, since I met her in January 2020. But I will elaborate.

During the study of Release the Dove, Rhonda "opened Scriptures" to me that I had known of for most of my life. But I didn't have the tools to unlock them in my life. I believed in miracles. I had even experienced some. Yet, I still was unsure of my position as a daughter, not just a creation, of the Most High God. This perspective changed my relationship with God. It fanned the flame of my soul. I have always loved Jesus and read the Word from childhood. Rhonda taught me, and is still teaching me, how to actively APPLY the Word. It's one thing to read "the Word of God is alive and active". It's another thing to experience it! Rhonda showed me how to experience the Word of God in a way that I hadn't before.

What makes this testimony of what Rhonda has sown into me so special, is that she is a grace gift to me. I didn't even know I needed her in my life. Upon meeting Rhonda initially, I fought with myself every week about whether or not I would return to the study she was teaching. The drive was about 45 minutes away from my home (one way) after work on a Tuesday. I didn't WANT to go. Yet, I was pulled back every week. By the end of study, I knew she had something that I hadn't experienced on a Sunday at any church I had ever attended. She had Holy Ghost Fire! I wanted that in my life!

Since submitting myself to Rhonda's mentorship, I have developed my prayer language, learned how to apply Scripture properly, and most importantly, my prayer life has gotten deeper. I am better equipped to pray for others and see results vs. praying and hoping that God heard my prayer. I hold my relationship with Rhonda very close to my heart. I pray that whoever reads this finds a mentor that will faithfully steward the sheep of the Lord as Rhonda has done for me.

Blessings,
Daria Morris

Daria's exponential Spiritual Growth is so evident!

I was chatting with Daria about how much her prayers had improved. Others on our platform had remarked about how poignant her prayers were. To the point of one sister taking Daria's prayer and reading it to her husband! This is just how incredibly transformed I have seen Daria in her spiritual walk with the Lord.

I've known her spiritual potential from the beginning and although I knew just how busy she was, I still entrusted her with leading the studying when I was away, teaching on various topics and this week she will be tag-teaming with another up-and-coming daughter in the faith, Kirsten. Daria's YES has always encouraged me. Without her knowing, I was observing to see just how much I could entrust her with, and she has returned repeatedly with the spirit of excellence.

These are some of Daria's Prayers from our Prayer Platform:

This prayer was for a mom who lost her 6-year-old son.

Jesus, Lord, You alone know why. Father, thank You that Your Word tells us that the righteous are taken away from evil. Holy Spirit, please comfort in the depths of this mama's soul. Vindicate her, O Lord by Your Righteous right hand. Your Word says that You revive, Lord. Revive this mama's heart and wrap her precious son, Your precious son in Your loving arms. God, I can't imagine! But we trust You. Your Word gives life and brings comfort. Jesus, You said blessed are those who mourn, for they shall be comforted. We believe You are true to Your Word, Father. We thank You for Your faithfulness.

A prayer in response to a request for a father suffering from urinary issues.

Father, we thank You for J. and for the heart of his precious daughter. Lord, thank You for giving us the authority to declare a thing in the earth and have it come to pass. We speak now to J's kidneys, bladder, ureters, and urethra. We command them to perform and function in the manner that You designed them to function! We bind infection, urine retention, and dysuria in the name of Jesus! We release freedom and wholeness in J's body and in his life. Your will is that we are free! You have proclaimed and paid for our freedom, Yeshua! We thank You that it IS done now in Your Name!

In response to a request where the individual was given only a few days to live if his situation did not improve.

Lord Jesus! We know that YOU alone have the final say in this matter, Lord. YOU have numbered our days, not physicians. You rule time, Father. They say two hours. Father, you can say two decades. In this moment, Holy Spirit, please strengthen this family to agree with You. Please calm this storm in the name of Jesus and help them to safely trust. In Jesus Name I pray. Amen.

Personal Reflections

Lupita's Re-story, USA
My Testimony

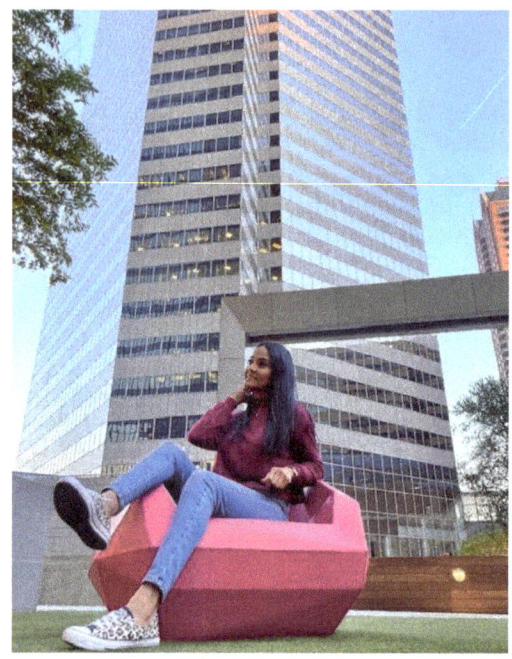

When I was a little girl growing up, I was not taught about the baptism of the Holy Spirit, I did not even know what the manifestation of speaking in tongues was. I didn't quite understand it, I thought of it as complicated and a mystery, so I neglected it until 2017 when I gave my life to God and began studying Scripture for myself. I was water baptized July 8th, 2018, and my heart's desire for the baptism of the Holy Spirit heightened, but I did not believe it to be possible for me.

In February of 2021, I was introduced to Mrs. Rhonda by one of the amazing ladies at my church. Three minutes into our conversation, I connected with her, her godly wisdom and soft spirit were so nurturing.

I honestly do not remember how the conversation about speaking in tongues arose, I heard excitement in her voice. She told me speaking in tongues was a promise of the Father and that if I asked for it, He (the Father) would do it! She embarked on this beautiful spiritual journey with me, she offered to walk me through receiving the gift of the Holy Spirit; I was full of joy.

We discussed what it meant for me to receive it, I purchased her _Release the Dove Workbook_, read, underlined what stood out to me and asked questions. She wanted to make sure I understood the meaning of receiving the Holy Spirit according to Jesus, not Mrs. Rhonda nor myself.

Acts 2:39 NIV spoke to my heart, *"This promise is to you, and to your children, and even to the Gentiles – all who have been called by the Lord our God."* I was in awe because as I stated earlier, I did not believe this was for me. Now I knew it *was,* but I did not feel worthy enough.

By faith I believed and envisioned a dove resting on me. This was the beginning. On February 26, 2021, we scheduled a Face-time call, I planned on fasting that day to intentionally deny my body's physical need for food and shift my focus towards faith and spirituality. I am not perfect, and there is beauty in that. I forgot to fast, and before I knew it, I was drinking coffee and having breakfast; no need to panic. God is not interested in perfection; He is a gracious and merciful God who knows my heart. Oh, what His peace and joy can do! Years back, I would have given up and judged myself; not this time, I am no longer a slave to the spirit of perfectionism.

I fasted lunch. I left work early to create a welcoming environment for the Holy Spirit, just like when we prepare for a house guest. I created a safe and intimate space. I had the house to myself, silenced my cell phone, closed the blinds, diffused a mixture of essential oils, and asked for the Holy Spirit to come in. Mrs. Rhonda and I went before the Father in prayer and asked Him to allow the Holy Spirit to release over my soul. As much as I would like to, I do not have words to describe this moment in its entirety. I was in a place of overflow in His presence, I felt full, lacking nothing. I opened my mouth and spoke what came out, it was not for me to make sense of the sound, I had to lean on my faith and not on my own understanding. What does make perfect sense to me now is Acts 2:4, *I was filled with the Holy Spirit and began to speak in tongues as the Spirit gave me utterance.*

It was a blessing to receive the baptism of the Holy spirit alongside a powerful woman of God. Mrs. Rhonda has been very instrumental in my faith journey; she is the Spiritual Mother my heart so longed for.

Beloved Sister Rhonda, Thank you.

Personal Reflections

Pastor Lisa Great's Re-story, USA

My Testimony

The day Mrs. Rhonda came into my life, was the day I began to be transformed into being a wife. This transformation is ongoing and even now after being married 10 years, I am still learning lessons from her wisdom that, to me, is a treasure money cannot buy. I was an independent single woman who came from a divorced family so was not aware of what it meant to be a wife.

When I got married, I thought I could navigate these waters of being a wife alone, but I quickly came to find out I had no navigational experience in these waters. This is when I sought the help of Mrs. Rhonda. A woman who had been married, successfully and cross-culturally for many years, became my compass who taught me how to be a wife.

I started my relationship with her sharing everything I thought was wrong with my husband, but very quickly I learned from her my responsibility is to be a wife not to worry about my husband.

Many tears have been shed over the years, but it was due to the loss of me and my way, to follow God and His way. Mrs. Rhonda is a Naomi to me, and I am her Ruth, whatever she says I do, for she has walked this road and I trust her implicitly. I have learned how to be a wife, a mother, a friend and so many other roles by following her lead. I learned to emote in the right places and right spaces; how to communicate with respect and honor, not anger, and disrespect. I learned how to die to myself so I could truly live for another.

God used Mrs. Rhonda to take this wild horse and break her so she could run the race set before her and win. I am forever grateful for Mrs. Rhonda's wisdom, counsel, correction, and consoling. She knew what I needed, when, and gave it to me. I have matured in ways only she knows, I have learned to be a wife and mother, both of which I thought I knew how to be until I got married. Thank you, Mrs. Rhonda, for investing in my family the way you do, I am truly grateful for you!

Hazel's Re-story, USA
My Testimony

I met Hazel at The Woodlands Church two years ago. The moderator asked the congregation to greet their neighbors. Hazel alone with her son, turned to greet Clement and myself. After service we chatted and found out we both had recently moved to Houston, and both lived in The Woodlands. Hazel invited me for coffee.

When I told my husband, he joked with me in French and said I'd better tell her my real age! I laughed at him, turning to Hazel I continued my conversation making sure she knew I had a grandson who was older than her son! Hazel did not act surprised and did not retract her invite for coffee!

She also joined me for my birthday celebration with three of my dear friends.

One day when I needed to catch a flight, Hazel offered to drive me. It was there that she confided in me how she had desired to have an older woman of color as a friend! She was looking for a spiritual Mom without even knowing what she truly sought!

Hazel, Emilio and I at The Woodlands Church shortly after meeting. The Baptismal pool is behind us.

I will let Hazel tell you in her own words.

"The day I met Rhonda; it was as if we had known each other forever. I know for a fact that I was placed in that precise moment in that precise place to meet my Spiritual Mother and to be blessed with her love, care, and words of wisdom. She is a woman with the strength of a warrior, but the heart of a mother, and she takes special care of each single one of her spiritual children. The only way I can make sense as to how she has so much energy to do all the beautiful things that she does, is because the Lord gives her the necessary strength to pursue his Word.

Rhonda is family to me and to my family, and I will forever be grateful to the Lord for blessing me with her presence in my life."

Hazel Macias,
Blessed

Hannelie's Re-story, South Africa
My Testimony

Hannelie is in red, alongside Andre her husband, Anzelle, son-n-law and Bernice.

Greetings dearest Rhonda. Praise God for He is good.
I am so glad that you have yet another book coming out to glorify our Father!!!

Our *'Upper Room'* meetings were as if one stepped onto Holy ground... Father, Spirit, Son all manifested in One (Trinity) when we met. Every time we prayed, I was slain in the Spirit, once I was out in the Spirit for almost 2 hours. I was strengthened, refreshed, and encouraged every time we met. I could not wait for us to meet, and I was expectant of what Abba would speak. God gave me promises in the *'Upper Room'* that have yet to be fulfilled but I believe that He is faithful, and His promises will surely come to pass.

Never in my life have I experienced the Lord's presence as I have experienced in our *'Upper Room'* Meetings. *It was absolutely amazing.*

How I wish that the Lord would use me also in such a mighty way to bring people closer to Him. To experience Him. To feel His love and to be encouraged to walk in the Spirit ... and know that He is with us, in us and that He wants to show Himself to those who truly seek Him with their whole heart.

My prayer for you Rhonda, is that Father will bless you even more. That He will use you in mighty ways, in ways that you have not even prayed about, thought about, or could even imagine. May the ripple effect of your obedience and faithfulness be more than anything you could fathom!!!

How often I wish that we could meet again and pray together. Not that one has to depend on feelings but when we met, I could feel the presence of our Lord. He showed up. He moves with you, Rhonda...He touches people through you.

In short, our *'Upper Room'* experiences were both amazing and real, we were in the Holy of Holies, where He touched us and spoke to us. Holy Spirit filled the room with His presence.

One can never ever be the same after such an experience...I am changed, and I am hungry for even more.

Much love dear Rhonda,

Hannelie (Andre, Anzelle and Bernice)

Esther's Re-story, The Netherlands

My Testimony – Running with Perseverance

I am the type of person who is always looking for new adventures and challenges to sign-up for, but at the same time, I get easily bored when the novelty wears off. As soon as that happens, I start looking for the next exciting adventure to conquer!

I love to participate in different sports in addition to several hobbies but seldom follow through with all these activities. Fortunately, I have my church community and my group of friends and family who provide a source of stability for me.

In the Fall of 2017, I was praying and asking for a new adventure that was in line with God's will and could be combined with my current job. Sometimes it's easy to seek adventures by going on a mission abroad and experience God very closely, but to have this adventure in your 'everyday' life might be more challenging. As I was praying, I happened to think of the upcoming Muskathlon in Jordan in the Fall of 2018. It was a fundraised marathon in a remote area to further the worldwide battle for justice. This would not only be a huge physical challenge (running 42,2 km), but also an enormous practical challenge (raising 10.000 euros)! I liked the idea but wasn't completely convinced.

Would I treat my body as a temple of God if I signed up for this extreme sport activity? Would it cause a huge impact on my body? Would I be able to raise so much money for injustice in a society very self-centered? Would I have time to train 4 times a week with a job and my sister's wedding coming up? Would my body have the stamina required to run such a long distance without me being an experienced runner? Would I be able to endure this journey if I am so easily bored? All these questions came up.

I took time to ponder on this great feat I was considering. I discussed this with friends and family. People liked the idea but came up with so many different reasons for me *NOT* to do it such as my body 'shape' wasn't meant to run. I had no experience, timing was bad, the set amount for fundraiser was too high and so on and so forth.

I was so discouraged to find that people had their opinions formulated before asking God Himself. They were so judgmental instead of taking my idea seriously and applauding me for considering partaking in this great cause.

I am a member of The Redeemer International Church family in The Hague, Netherlands and Rhonda was one of my *Spiritual Mothers* there. I went to her seeking for some wise counsel. She told me that if God told me so and it was in line with Scripture, I should do it! I had her blessing, and she was willing to support me in the journey!

This was so controversial to the advice I had received before, that I was shocked! She explained *'the principle of the three'*, that I had to ask two others for confirmation and if I received their blessing as well, I should sign-up (2 Corinthians 13:3). Besides, if it were God's will for me to run this race, He would provide in every way and that 10.000 euros was nothing to Him.

So, I went to ask two other spiritual mothers and they both prayed as well and saw no reason why *I shouldn't do it,* therefore I signed up in the beginning of 2018! I was so nervous and couldn't see how God would help me run 42 km and would provide 10.000 euros, but I decided to trust Him.

I started training with a running schedule, designed my fundraiser page and shared the news of this exciting adventure with the people around me. I had to make sacrifices in not seeing my friends as often as I would love to, because training was my priority now. Like I told you, I tend to become so easily bored, so running for a few hours seemed boring to me! Since I felt it was my divine assignment, I asked God for a solution. He started speaking to me personally during those trainings and I had my quiet time during my runs. I would listen to podcasts and music but was mostly praying, discussing, and enjoying my conversations with Jesus. He really filled me up with joy during those moments. I was so excited that even when I was unable to run, instead I would jump and dance! My heart was overflowing with joy, and I loved Jesus' company.

As the training schedule became more intense, I started having little pains, I couldn't discern what was a 'good' pain and which one was a 'bad' pain. So, I joined a running club and used this opportunity to share my motivation to run this race glorifying Jesus. People were skeptical: how could I run a marathon with so little experience? Of course, this made me doubt even the more (after all, they were the professionals) but I trusted God to do a miracle and that He would provide, because it was His plan anyway!

Also, during this time Rhonda prophesied Hebrews 12:1-3 NIV over me, which says, *"Therefore, since we are surrounded by such a great cloud of witnesses, let us throw off everything that hinders and the sin that so easily entangles. And let us run with perseverance the race marked out for us, ² fixing our eyes on Jesus, the pioneer and perfecter of faith. For the joy set before him he endured the cross, scorning its shame, and sat down at the right hand of the throne of God. ³ Consider him who endured such opposition from sinners, so that you will not grow weary and lose heart."*

The phrase *'running the race with perseverance'* jumped out at me. Rhonda told me that although I would be running in the natural, I'd also be running in the spiritual. God really unraveled this Scripture to me and the importance of the cloud of witnesses cheering you on, fixing our eyes on Jesus and the end goal, and not losing heart by negative comments or other obstacles. This Scripture became my mantra and helped me to keep going and stay focused! It gave me a deeper meaning as I saw it both in the natural and spiritual and still helps me to cheer others on in their own race of life.

The money was a different issue. In my culture, people might find it annoying when you ask for money and with that in mind, I couldn't think of a way to 'beg' for 10.000 euros for a far-away cause (Christian Iraqi refugees who fled from Islamic State (IS) and are now based in Jordan). Also, it seems easier to raise funds for a general poverty cause instead of persecuted Christians, particularly to your non-Christian friends!

However, Rhonda loves fundraisers and was my biggest cheerleader. She offered to organize my fundraiser and I was so pleased. So many people contributed for the food, location, music, auction, fun activity and so on. After the fundraiser I wanted to cover those costs, but no one accepted the money – it was all donated. All glory to God – with this one event I raised around 7.000 euros for the fundraiser, and we were on our knees! My faith was soaring, and God really proved that He is Jehovah Jireh – the God who provides.

The last bit of money came in from different sources, very unexpectedly. People I relied on didn't donate, people I didn't count on donated a lot. God was working in His miraculous way and His ways proved to be so much higher than my thinking! Within 6 months I had all the money fundraised and could fully focus on my training.

However, people still wanted to donate, even when I explained to them that I had reached my target, therefore it was not necessary. Still, they didn't accept my explanation, instead they questioned me about my travel expenses. Yes, that wasn't paid yet but I had planned to cover my flight and accommodations during my stay in Jordan. People were so overwhelmingly generous and would not take 'no' for an answer----their donations flooded in. Well! I was flabbergasted and couldn't understand how God was providing above and beyond!

I had full confidence in this journey now. Money was covered, I saw the results of my training and could totally see the marathon happening. People around me were encouraging and I could testify at my work about Jesus – using the marathon as a conversation starter.

I had found a good balance and enjoyed the ride now! Only the last bit of the training schedule was dubious, having to run very long distances, getting the final training done before the resting period began.

I learned that during the last weeks before a marathon, you don't train so much anymore, as you give your body time to recover and be full on for the race! But in these last weeks of intense training (which were the most important and getting you ready to run the 42km) I sustained an injury. I was so discouraged and didn't understand how this could happen! I was so focused and found a good balance and only a few more weeks of training remained! Rhonda had encouraged me to contact Nicole earlier who gave me lots of advice! She had cycled from Italy to Holland and was not only encouraging but enthusiastic about my run.

I was crying out to God, why? He revealed I had become prideful. Instead of relying on Him as I did from the start, I was trusting in my trained body and boasting in myself. It brought me back on to my knees. I knew now that only God could sustain me during this race. Without these last weeks of training and without a full focus I really didn't know how I could run a marathon in a desert area in a foreign country. I was so down and out. Praying didn't heal me in that moment and I could just only trust that God would do a miracle during the race. I gave up on super healthy food, focused training and went discouraged and anxious on the flight to Jordan. Only God could do it now.

I soon found out the team I was running with all had their own stories and needed faith for a miracle. One had had her cecum (a pouch that forms the first part of the large intestine) removed recently, one couldn't run because of a severe bee bite, another was serving in a refugee camp and had no time to train and so on. I didn't have the worst story after all with my injury! Some were in excellent shape but were encouraging that we're in this together, and God had performed so many miracles, thus far, we could expect Him to move now as well.

And He did... Even during the race when wild dogs started chasing me and I didn't dare to run past them, I was praying for a solution that God would send someone from my team at that moment to join me. Or when I was running up a steep hill (remember I trained in flat Holland), I asked God to help me accomplish that mountain. In that moment He showed me the faces of the kids we visited during that week, and I started praying for them. Before I finished all the prayers for the kids I was on top of the hill!

So many stories within this story. Also, my injury wasn't too bad during the race. I was enjoying the run and the time I had with God. Before I knew it, I heard people chanting my name. I didn't understand why until I saw I was about to finish the race. I had so much energy left (can you imagine?) on this spiritual high that I could run an extra loop! I finished the race with a huge smile and as the second woman! I can only say: God worked a miracle and will finish what He has started within you.

Thank you, Rhonda – for cheering me on in this spiritual and physical journey – I learned so many lessons and it has built my faith for the rest of my life.

Esther Pot,
The Netherlands

Dorothy's Re-story, USA
Rhonda as my Spiritual Mother, sister, and friend
My Testimony

In September 2014, our family was transferred from Rio De Janeiro, Brazil to Kuala Lumpur (KL), Malaysia. As we arrived and began settling into our new lives, I naturally had to deal with the challenges of moving to a new city and discovering a new culture. At the time, my "spiritual tank" was dry, and I knew that I needed to grow under the mentorship of a godly Christian woman.

On a faithful October evening, I attended a parents' meeting at my children's school and at the end of the meeting, I met a lady who gave me a ride home. It happened that we lived in the same apartment building (the Lord's orchestration). On our drive home, she talked to me about Sister Rhonda, as well as the Oasis Women's Fellowship. She said, "I will introduce you to Sister Rhonda, and she will bring you to the ladies' fellowship." Later, I spoke to Sister Rhonda, and it happened that she literally lived across the street from me, I could see her apartment from mine. A few days after, Sister Rhonda invited me to Oasis and gave me a ride to my first meeting, and many more to come. While riding in the car with her, I immediately got drawn to how much she loved the Lord. Little did I know that she was the mentor that I prayed for.

Sister Rhonda and I grew into each other. We always went to the women's fellowship together, and I was always blessed by the timely word of God that she shared. After fellowship, we had to hang around a while before leaving, as there were always women waiting to get counsel or be prayed for by Sister Rhonda. I felt she had so much wisdom and I was gleaning as much as I could and as fast as I could.

In the Summer of 2015, my eldest sister, the late Mrs. Barbara Amego who had been like a mom to me, came to visit me in KL. I had been telling Barbara about Sister Rhonda and she was happy to finally meet her, only to realize she had met Sis. Rhonda years ago, in a women's fellowship in Warri, Nigeria. Before my sister traveled back to Nigeria, she said to me, *"I am no longer worried about you, with Sister Rhonda on your side, you'll be fine."* Sadly, four months later, my sister went home to be with the Lord.

Sister Rhonda became a mom, a mentor, sister, and trusted friend all in one. She has been a huge blessing in my life. Indeed, words cannot describe all that she means to me. She prays for me, and with me, she has walked the journey that I'm still embarking on and always has godly wisdom to give. She has been a blessing even to my children, so much that whenever we have some important matter on the table, my 22-year-old daughter often asks "Mom, have you told Sister Rhonda?" The amazing thing is that Sister Rhonda loves people. She allows everyone to occupy a special place in her heart and I'm yet to understand how she's able to do that.

Sister Rhonda has been and continues to be my mentor and spiritual Mom. We both currently live in Houston, and it has been too wonderful knowing she's just a few miles from me. I love you, Sister Rhonda. May the Lord continue to bless you and use you for His glory in the mighty name of Jesus, Amen.

Photo taken in my home in Kuala Lumpur. L to R: Miriam, Dorothy, and her mom, myself with Barbara's newborn and beautiful Barbara on the right.

Being Jesus in the Marketplace

"So, he was reasoning in the synagogue with the Jews and the God-fearing Gentiles, and in the market place every day with those who happened to be present," Acts 17:17 NIV.

A Divine Encounter

My husband has this assiduous way in ensuring that I am included in every business transaction, on every Bank account and every house signing there is! He means well but I trust him to handle all our finances!

This occasion was no different. He had decided we needed to open a joint account at a particular Bank, despite the fact I was quite happy doing banking at the same Bank where I had been for the last 35 years.

Nevertheless, he booked an appointment on a Saturday morning, the day I'd usually be at my newly joined Gym and Spa he gifted me with for my birthday. I was pulling on my gym clothes when he announced in his usual impromptu manner that we had an appointment at the bank and needed to get going.

I scowled at this news, exchanging my gym clothes for a dress, and followed him to his car regretting my Body Pump class that I would miss. We chatted in the car but were careful not to get distracted and to keep an eye open for the sign of the bank.

We were new to The Woodlands. The name really depicts the scenery in the area. As The Netherlands never ceased to amaze me by having a restaurant in the middle of a forest, The Woodlands held the same charm. Woods lined the streets and highways, there were signs of what lay beyond, but one had to be attentive, so as not to bypass the area, especially if you were accustomed to seeing buildings and businesses as you passed. After a short while of searching, we finally found the bank tucked in an inconspicuous area of the woods.

I took a last glance at my appearance in the mirror before I exited my husband's vehicle. I wanted to make sure I was presentable. Instantly, my hands went to smoothing the wrinkles out of my dress. I wanted to make a good impression at the bank. My husband and I are both old-school, we try to always dress appropriately for every occasion.

We were met by a pretty blonde who led us to her office. After some pleasantries, we settled on which accounts would work best and she started completing the paperwork on-line. The process was going smoothly when my husband's phone rang, and he had to excuse himself to go outside the office to take the call. He squeezed my shoulder gently excusing himself.

Still feeling a bit annoyed with my husband for intruding on my Saturday morning, I continued light conversation with the young lady, when I looked up and was startled to find this beautiful blonde with tears rolling down her cheeks as she began to pour her heart out to me. She told me how she and her husband had a son and desired to have a second child. They had recently suffered a miscarriage, yet she had an ardent desire to have a second child. I quickly transitioned into counseling mode, encouraging her and received a Word from God on the spot for her situation. I told her MOST definitely that she would have a child. I encouraged her to trust in the Lord.

Shortly afterwards, my husband returned apologizing for this lapse of time. Janice and I (not her real name) exchanged smiles as she quickly regained her composure and completed our application.

Fast forward two years later, I received a letter in the mail informing me that the bank branch would be closing, and I would need to remove items from my safety deposit box. Days went by before I could contact the bank about this matter. The same blonde whom I had met two years earlier at that divine appointment, answered the call. She remembered me and filled in the gaps since we had seen one another.

She had called her mom that same day we had met, to tell her about our encounter. "Mom," she cried, "Do you really think I can have another child?" Her mother answered without hesitation, "Nothing is impossible with God."

Janice joined her faith with mine and with her husband's. They had both decided they would try IVF as that would be the only way they could conceive, so they thought.

"Let's start eating healthy and exercising," Rick suggested (not his real name). He wanted to ensure that they were as healthy as possible to prepare for a rigorous cycle of IVF which happens to be mentally and physically draining. As they were consistent in this new regiment, Janice noticed that her husband was losing weight, but she seemed to be gaining. She thought, how odd!

After further investigation into the matter, they found out only a few months after our divine encounter, Janice was expecting their bundle of Joy! Leah was born one day before her beloved grandfather's birthday.

Rick and Janice had been so excited when their delivery date was the same as her grandfather's birthday! What a sweet omen, a propitious outcome, she thought.

Leah might have been born on his birthday if not for the fact that her doctor needed to induce the pregnancy. A short four months later when she lost her grandfather, she understood fully the mercies of our God. It would have been a bittersweet affair if the baby would have come on the date as planned.

The day I went into the bank to handle the matter of my safety deposit box, I made it a point to stop by Janice's office before leaving. Again, it was a divine encounter. She showed me gorgeous photos of her little angel.
I gazed at beautiful Leah with her bouncy blonde curls and round oval eyes and could not help but to thank Almighty God for His blessings upon this grateful couple.

As we chatted, we found out we attended the same church! She had been married at our church!

Before leaving, I was prompted to tell her she would have another child. She told me she had dreamed of that as well but had her tubes tied. She had desired to adopt a child and was almost given a child by a random person in a grocery store ten years earlier! That desire had never ceased! Indeed, nothing is impossible with God!

A Contractor's Encounter with Jesus

Arriving home from overseas was always exhausting for me, not sleeping on the plane coupled with the list of many things needed to be done at home BEFORE I could even get on with the joy of visiting family.

We had received a letter from our Home Association about getting our house painted. So, first thing on the list was to find a contractor. I looked for a few contractors and there were some, also that my husband recommended by looking on a Home Improvement site. I had asked my Property Manager to be present for the quotations as I felt contractors would try to take advantage of me being a woman.

The very first contractor arrived in our home and began to praise the beautiful décor and asked if I had had it professionally done. I explained to him the different objects that he questioned me about from places I had visited. Then seemingly from nowhere, he broke down in tears. He told me he felt God's presence and knew I was a woman of God. He did not plan to cheat me but wanted to be honest about his quotation.

Both my Property Manager and I were stunned about his display of emotion and admitting what I had already felt in my heart. I knew that God had touched him to do right by me! After reviewing other quotations, he was the one we chose to do the job!

The Berean Study Bible says in Proverbs 1:3-4, *"All a man's ways are pure in his own eyes, but his motives are weighed out by the LORD. ³Commit your works to the LORD and your plans will be achieved. ⁴The LORD has made everything for His purpose—even the wicked for the day of disaster."*

A Contractor Chosen by God

After many years of using our home as a Summer Home whilst we lived overseas, we decided to rent it out. We chose what we thought would be a suitable family.

Our home was a blessed one having seen the glory of God upon our purchase ten years earlier. Both Clement and I had sat at the empty fireplace and felt this was to be our haven in the States. A light had shone from the top window of this gorgeous house bathing us in sunlight. We both sat in hushed silence for a long while. The realtor had joined us at the hearth but also sat quietly during this sacred moment. After viewing so many homes, we knew this one was ours.

The neighborhood was called HavenStone and it was secluded in a beautiful area of Snellville, Georgia. Our home was nestled in a gated community, hidden away from the hustle and bustle which could be present in a city so close to Atlanta.

We enjoyed coming home to the States and inviting friends and family to share our blessed haven with us. After over ten years of living this lifestyle, we decided we would rent our precious property.

Our new Property Manager handled the process expertly as we were away. She treated our home as if it were hers. She found a family whom she felt would be reliable and who would keep our home safe.

We had one of the biggest companies in America handling our rental property in addition to our Property Manager. Unfortunately, a hurricane hit, and the rental company was unable to keep up with all their clients. Our tenants gave less than a two weeks' notice and breeched the contract. Not only was this a travesty but they left our home with cosmetic damage that took hundreds of dollars of repair!

Our first rental experience caused my heart to bleed. I had to have a paradigm shift in my mindset to survive. It felt like a violation to our peaceful sweet haven called home.

Again, finding contractors was high on the list. The first one who came drove a Hummer and I knew that we would not be able to afford him, yet he promised me that his prices would be lower than all the rest of the bids! He was right! He made himself available to do all the cosmetic work at a low rate and showed myself and our Property Manager how to do many small jobs ourselves!

But most importantly, he shared valuable lessons on how to rent property, and taught me an indispensable lesson: that I should no longer consider this property as my home but as rental space. Detaching my heart from it proved harder than one would expect but once I did, it made all the difference!

Ed remained in our lives beyond that home and helped with another rental space even agreeing to go to court with me, as I later needed to do, with a renter in default.

When there was no-one available to pick up our son from the airport, he volunteered to do so. He even extended his advice to helping my son with our car and so much more. God put him in our lives for that time and I will never ever forget that. He also told me that I reminded him of an aunt who prayed a lot. I believe he also felt that he had been sent to us because he often said, "I've got your back." When others tried to get him to do work, he was not available, yet he remained constant for us! To God be all the Glory!

My Property Manager, Wanda, was even more dedicated than Ed, as if that could be possible! From the moment she took on the job, our home became hers! Before renting our home, we had to pack everything up. I was working in Holland and not able to travel to America, so my husband did. Yet Wanda organized the entire move and even packed most of the things herself!

I was always so touched; no amount of money could pay for the peace of mind that she gave us. I was overwhelmed by the goodness of our Lord through her. The Lord reminded me of the many times I had done the exact same things for others. He let me know that I was simply reaping what I had sown and that for sure, Wanda would do the same!

Colossians 3:23-24 NIV
[23] "Whatever you do, work at it with all your heart, as working for the Lord, not for human masters, [24] since you know that you will receive an inheritance from the Lord as a reward. It is the Lord Christ you are serving."

Pete - Omni Construction

We live in a beautiful home in Texas; however, fitting our furniture and treasured pieces from around the world proves to be a difficult task to do tastefully. My husband refers to our home as a 'museum', and I truly hope one day it will be! Our travels have been so very special that I savor the moment when guests arrive, and I get to share experiences through the pieces scattered around our home. These treasures tell of our history and the rich lives the Lord has blessed us to live.

Our plan to add stairs to the garage to get to our attic, rapidly transformed into an "Upper Room" once we saw the attic space available to us. My husband wanted to move his office up there to give me more room downstairs. We used a contractor who had helped us earlier that year. I had been amazed that he was the owner and came to build shelves above my garage on his day off! But this was in line with Pete's character! An honest and humble soul who quickly became a friend to my husband and me. The name of his company is Omni which means 'in all places'. Truly God has expanded his business in so many places and areas, yet Pete treats a billion-dollar project just as he would a $1000 dollar one, meticulously and showing grace and attention to each client. After each job, he sends a book entitled "The Story" which tells the Bible in story book form. This is one way he gets to spread the Gospel of Jesus Christ.

One day when he came over to look at plans for our 'Upper Room' space, his eyes shone and glistened and were dancing with excitement! He asked to see my husband and me. Thinking this concerned our building project, I interrupted my husband's meeting (he has been working from home mostly since 2020).

What Pete wanted to discuss was much more important than building a room, it had to do with building lives! He told us how he had shared Jesus with a client yesterday. He was humbled to see how the Lord used him in this manner. The client had an addiction and the Lord allowed Pete to see through that addiction and get to his soul. Pete shared the love of God with him and had the inclination to return from his car and pray for the client! Since then, the client has attended Church and his life has been turned around by one man's obedience to share the Gospel in the marketplace!

On another occasion as Pete was leaving our home, I mentioned to him that I had a baptism to do but no place to do it. Without hesitation, he offered to heat his pool in the dead of Winter! He and I had the opportunity to baptize a father and a son in those baptismal waters! But not before Pete shared his life-changing testimony with them!

Pete had been a millionaire in his twenties, but like the Prodigal Son, he squandered all his money, only to return home to his parents, dejected and broke. After wallowing for over five years in his sorrow, misery and regret for his sin, God spoke to him, and Pete listened. He repented and was transformed by the power of Almighty God. He had a rare second chance to rebuild his life and his business. God has been exceedingly good to Pete, and he does not hesitate to spread that goodness to others around him. Again, we were able to see transformation of lives at its finest! Our God is awesome!

I marvel at the provision of God and how he has made us bold for his Kingdom if we would only obey!

Poems and Sacred Reflections

The Birth of my Grandson Olivier

Standing in the Labor Room praying for Olivier to come into this world and anticipating the joy this life would bring. Lord I'm weary. Alesea is weary. My first-born wanted to deliver drug-free, but the wait is too long and the pain too great! *"In my desperation I prayed, and the Lord listened; He saved me from all my troubles."* Psalm 34:6 NLT.

T.D. Jakes has a "Woman Thou Art Loosed" Conference in Atlanta that I'm scheduled to be at tomorrow. My friends will be coming from Gabon, Africa to join me at this event, my thoughts ran rampant.

We are waiting, anticipating. Mel, my son-in-law, paces the floor, wringing his hands, not knowing what to do to alleviate Alesea's pain.

"I'm going for chicken wings at Walmart next door," I said, needing to get out of that space into the fresh air. Walking to my car, still calling on the Lord to intervene, I throw up my hands towards Heaven.

Errand run, back at the hospital, things have accelerated, and Life is about to arrive! Thank you, Lord. *"For His anger is fleeting, but His favor lasts a lifetime. Weeping may stay the night, but joy comes in the morning."* Psalm 30:5, The Berean Study Bible.

Infinity Love

So tiny and so precious and beautiful is he,
who would ever believe that this angel was sent to me?

You came much too soon, we were totally caught by surprise,
Yet when you appeared in our world on August 3rd,
Pain and fears subside.

I love you more than anything, and I will always pray
That the Lord would grant you peace and in His perfect will you stay.
I pray that the Lord would guide and protect you,
And keep you through the storms of life —

Help you when you stumble
Keep you away from strife.
So just how much do you love me, Koko?
I'm sure one day you may ask.
Infinity x2

Forever and always!

Written by Rhonda Wilson-Dikoko following the birth of her Grandson whom she named Olivier. Aug 3, 2005

Be Still and know that I am God
A reflection from "Release the Dove Book" during Olivier's convalescence

Psalms 46:10 NIV:
He says, *"Be still, and know that I am God; I will be exalted among the nations, I will be exalted in the earth."*

Lord, though you have commanded that I be still and KNOW that you are God, so many things are clamoring for my attention. As I sit down to spend time in your presence, the phone beeps, my 'to do' list is begging for my attention, I need to write the recap for our Oasis meeting, I must check Olivier's temperature, he's going to miss school again today.

Lord, being still, in this cosmopolitan fast-paced world we live, can be an impossible feat to master, yet you command: Be Still, so *Be Still I must*!
In the still quietness, your presence is palpable. I relax my stance and fall to my knees. This is so familiar to me and truly where my soul has longed to be!
"*Eli, Eli, lama sabachthani?*" (Which means "My God, my God, why have you forsaken me?" Matthew 27:46 NIV). I have waited on you, I have cried out to you, I have longed for your presence!

You say in Psalms 27:8 NIV *"Seek my face..."*, Lord, it is your face I now seek! Show me your ways so that I might be used by thee.

My grandson is ill, the doctors are remiss on which route to take. The process of getting results back from England is lengthy; Lord, I need a move, a word from you! my desperate cries fill the room.

As I lay on the floor, now prostrate, tear-stained face, totally oblivious to my surroundings, completely at home with the Lord, I pour my heart out to God. Abba Father. Inaudible, indistinguishable words gush out from my innermost being as I pour out my heart and spirit to Him (Romans 8:26).

"He knows the way that I will take, and when He gets through with me, I shall come forth as pure gold" (Job 23.10 NIV).

I lie on the floor and slowly pull myself up in a sitting position, back supported by the bed. I listen and the Lord speaks.

A poem for Mother's Day – The Heart of a Woman
Mitema ya Basi

The heart of a woman, not easy to pry,
Insist husbands become spies,
The heart belies her innermost desires.
Not always reflecting the Spirit's cry.

Our hearts articulate like a rose,
Which but opens and close.
Reclusive in pain,
Hurt because of the shame.
Eager to love when loved in return,
Heart always yearns....
Mitema ya Basi

A woman is strong, determined, and shrewd,
like Jael who took down King Sisera single-handedly
or Deborah, a Judge in Israel.

What about Esther who delivered
her people by her bravery?
or Hannah who birthed a priest?
Who has seen the likes of Mary Magdalene?
who was first to carry the Gospel?
Or the woman at the well who understood worship?

And my favorite, Abigail, whose wisdom
spared her foolish husband Nabal.
Mary, who gave birth to Jesus,
the Savior of humanity.

Little is known about Dorcas, who
made lovely garments yet imbibed no vanity.
Eve coerced her husband to eat forbidden fruit.
Causing mankind to uproot.... from the Garden of Eden.

What is it that these women have in common?
Their traits quite Phenomenal.

All were redeemed by the Lord,
purpose fulfilled on earth.
Wise as a serpent and harmless as a dove,
receiving their mandates from above.

The Heart of a woman, is a beautiful thing,
But it is her spirit that has been redeemed.

Born of water, gone through fire,
Dressed in her finest attire.
Ready to give and all but reveal,
the secret to her divine success,
not giving in to any of the devil's tests.
Tenacious in spirit and ever creating life,
Enduring much sacrifice,
Forging ahead to reach her goal,
Her future having been foretold.

She is woman, she is strong
despite of the wrongs, done to her.
She still loves, forgives, and births humanity,
Mitema ya Basi.

Written By Rhonda Wilson Dikoko for Mother's Day TAIC (*The Ambassador's International Church in Kuala Lumpur Malaysia*), 2015

Joy Cometh – Winter 2017, The Hague, The Netherlands

Usually, I walk to work from the bus stop with a cloak of darkness enveloping me. The world is not yet awake. There is nothing but darkness and stillness. During those times I lift my voice and recite Psalms 23 out loud. Underfoot can be heard brittle twigs and icy grass. No other audible sound is detected in the dawn of the woods.

1 "The Lord is my shepherd; I shall not want.
2   He makes me lie down in green pastures.
He leads me beside still waters.[a]
3   He restores my soul.
He leads me in paths of righteousness[b]
*   for his name's sake.*
4 Even though I walk through the valley of the shadow of death,[c]
*   I will fear no evil,*
for you are with me;
*   your rod and your staff,*
*   they comfort me.*
5 You prepare a table before me
*   in the presence of my enemies;*
you anoint my head with oil;
*   my cup overflows.*
6 Surely goodness and mercy shall follow me
*   all the days of my life,*
and I shall dwell in the house of the Lord
*   forever."*

I mumble this prayer under my breath.

This morning my path was bathed with light. Reminds me of the Scripture, "... weeping lasts for a night but there's a song of joy in the morning..." (God's Word). Through a snow-strewn pathway winding through sleepy neighborhoods, dawn awakes. February enveloped in snow seems a faux pas of Nature, yet God in His infinite wisdom is up to something.

Lifting our hearts and bringing light to our darkened pathways. *"Weeping may endure for a night, but joy cometh in the morning..."* (Psalms 30:5 NIV).

No regrets, Winter 2017

People come and go.

I met her at the bus stop, her name was Shawn Powers. We exchanged pleasantries and because we met so often, we spoke more frequently as well.

I learned she had been living in The Netherlands for over 20 years and now was awaiting retirement. She had not married and had no children. Her Mom had died a year earlier; she only had a distant sister. Shawn Powers was biding her time for the day she would retire and receive her pension. This is when she would begin to live.

She had a furry brown hat like mine. Like those they wear in Russia in the dead of Winter. My friend Cynthia had made fun of mine, but it kept my head warm and was elegant to wear. I noticed how Shawn wore hers with such dignity, I wore mine more often after that.

This particular morning was odd. It was perhaps the coldest day of the Winter. I wore my hat and thought of Shawn's warning to walk gingerly on the icy ground to prevent a fall. She had told of how she had hired a ride sometimes to drop her at work because of the treacherous path. I thought of her now and heeded her caution.

Walking on that darkened path, my heart began to thump and race. The shadows of the trees played tricks on my mind. The fierce wind blew as the rain from the trees fell on my furry hat. I was glad I had worn it. I could not understand my fear. With every footstep, I heard Shawn's voice of conversations past. Arriving at work, I found she had gone.

Just like that! A colleague, that I had met at the bus stop, held conversation, and anticipated inviting her to Thanksgiving dinner, was gone!

How could knowing someone for such a short time produce such a measure of grief? I was grief-stricken and did not bother to hide this from our colleagues. Perhaps because she lived a life of regrets. The most pitiful thing is that she had no-one to weep for her. Her life was unfinished and there would surely be regrets about how she had lived it, just waiting, and biding her time. I mourned for this sweet lady knowing there would be few who would. I was given space to mourn. Life should be lived with no regrets.

The Day my Heart bled, yet there was nary a pain
('Nary' is African American slang for 'no' or 'none')

It came by way of email. The means of communication of this day and age. Much has changed in the world we live in. I had been busy all morning with important calls. One with a friend concerning fertility issues and one with another regarding her marriage. So preoccupied in conversation was I, that a glance at the clock reminded me of my 2:40 pm Dermatology appointment. It was now 2.40 pm! I quickly concluded the call.

Wasting valuable time in two attempts to phone the clinic, I decided to just show up and wait; even if I did not go to the appointment, I would still have to pay. At the bus stop, I finished tidying my appearance, combed my hair and put on a touch of lipstick but no make-up on my face. I wanted the doctor to be able to make a proper diagnosis of my skin issues.

The bus arrived. I hopped on, finding a place near the door. I prayed a silent prayer to still make my appointment in time. I fiddled with my phone going through emails, the usual routine while on the bus. Yet there was NOTHING usual about today!

Then I saw it. I saw the email. The one that caused my heart to bleed yet stay in perfect peace (Isaiah 26:3). I read through it once, then closed my phone. I looked out the window at this beautiful day the Lord had bestowed upon us. Unusual blue skies and beautiful Spring weather. My mind wandered to Jackie Onassis and Coretta Scot King. Both have been commended for their regal statues, ability to remain private despite of being in constant public scrutiny. I sighed. The news I had just read, had the capacity to turn my world upside down into Winter blues... if not for the grace of God. My eldest child had texted to find out if I had heard. I said I had. She wanted to know my state of mind. I told her I was fine and gave her comforting and encouraging words.

Hurrying to the clinic I glanced across the street and to my amazement gazed upon these words written on a building. It was a poem by Emily Dickenson:

Yesterday is History,
'Tis so far away
Yesterday is Poetry
'Tis Philosophy

Yesterday is mystery
Where it is Today
While we shrewdly speculate
Flutter both away.

My God, you do have a sense of humor, I chuckled! A few years earlier, this news would have set a negative movement into motion. A short decade ago, my future would have been sealed by this knowledge. I would have been frantic, upset and crying. Yet here I was showing up late for a doctor's appointment. Should the fact be told, I was more upset about being late than about the mind-boggling email I had just read! Excuse the cliché: I was as cool as a cucumber!

I have a Bible App on my phone. The Word for today was: "But if we walk in the light, as He is in the light, we have fellowship one with another and the blood of Jesus His Son cleanses us from all sin" (1 John 1:7 KJV). So, fitting.

The previous day's Scripture read, John 16:33 Amplified Bible:

33 "I have told you these things, so that in Me you may have [perfect] peace. In the world you have tribulation and distress and suffering, but be courageous [be confident, be undaunted, be filled with joy]; I have overcome the world. [My conquest is accomplished, My victory abiding.]"

Classic! Our God is a personal God who steps down to us, rolls up his sleeves and gets into our situations. That was it! My fate was sealed in Christ! I chose to believe His Word.

The next day was Bible Study in my home. I had set the stage with scented candles in the stairwell leading up to our apartment, table set for two since the majority of the members would be absent today. I had asked my youngest to lend us her guitar again, since the young lady coming is a worshiper.

What a set-up! God had planned my day! The others being absent was not a mishap but carefully orchestrated by God. I had my own private worship service with the Lord. At first, I sang along with Viki until I could not hold my composure any longer. I lay prostrate on the floor pouring out my heart to the Lord while Viki continued to play in melodious tones, oblivious to my bleeding heart. I heard Danielle join in song, but I lay in the presence of God until my human heart which had been pierced, was tended to.

Abba Father truly loves us and sings over us as it reads in Zephaniah 3:17 NIV.

The Word today was from:

Hebrews 6:10 GOD'S WORD Translation -- "God is fair. He won't forget what you've done or the love you've shown for him. You helped his holy people, and you continue to help them."

What makes this Scripture so meaningful to me, is that God had given me this Scripture as a Rhema Word over 21 years ago, while standing on the balcony of my Pointe Noire home in Congo (when I questioned Him about my future). So today was a reminder from God that my future is assured ONLY in Him.

If you are reading this today and you have doubts whether God knows or cares about the affairs of your life, wonder no longer! He cares so much, friend! *"Cast your cares on the LORD and he will sustain you; he will never let the righteous be shaken."* (Psalms 55:22 NIV).

Eternity Speaks

Standing on the balcony of my friend Tina's home which borders Geneva, you can see Mont Blanc. This snow-capped wonder served as an assurance to me that indeed our God reigns. He who created the world never sleeps nor slumbers. When I see the magnificent beauty of Creation whether it is Mont Blanc, The Grand Canyons or The Kilimanjaro, I am reminded of the Greatness that our God alone carries. I am in awe and speechless at the work of His hands. Job describes it in chapter 38 NIV. A few verses are cited here, but you must read the full chapter to understand the Magnificent indescribable scope of our Creator God.

"What is the way to the abode of light?
 And where does darkness reside?
[20] Can you take them to their places?
 Do you know the paths to their dwellings?
[21] Surely you know, for you were already born!
 You have lived so many years!
[22] Have you entered the storehouses of the snow
 or seen the storehouses of the hail,
[23] which I reserve for times of trouble,
 for days of war and battle?
[24] What is the way to the place where the lightning is dispersed,
 or the place where the east winds are scattered over the earth?
[25] Who cuts a channel for the torrents of rain,
 and a path for the thunderstorm,
[26] to water a land where no one lives,
 an uninhabited desert,
[27] to satisfy a desolate wasteland
 and make it sprout with grass?
[28] Does the rain have a father?
 Who fathers the drops of dew?
[29] From whose womb comes the ice?
 Who gives birth to the frost from the heavens
[30] when the waters become hard as stone,
when the surface of the deep is frozen?"

We don't just write songs for the sake of words, but we must be prolific, as Nicole Mullen expresses in her timeless rendition of "My Redeemer Lives" in the first stanza:

Who taught the sun where to stand in the morning?
And who told the ocean, you can only come this far?

And who showed the moon where to hide 'til evening?
Whose words alone can catch a falling star?
Well, I know my Redeemer lives
I know my Redeemer lives
All of creation testifies
This life within me cries
I know my Redeemer lives, yeah!

Chris Tomlin captures it in "Great God", yet none of these songs or passages can truly depict the grandeur or the majesty of our God. My heart bursts with unspeakable joy to even think about it. My spirit longs for the day I can behold His glory face to face. Though my carnal mind cannot conceive that notion, my spirit has captured it already. There is a knowing that is there, which cannot be erased. We were made for Eternity. These bodies are corrupt but will be made one day incorruptible.

Eternity speaks to me of words from the Eternal One. One glance at Mont Blanc reminds me of what a strong tower we have in our Lord. It says in Proverbs 18:10 ESV -- *"The Name of the Lord is a strong tower; the righteous man runs into it and is safe."* Saved from destruction, sickness, depression, failed marriages, lost children, and gone too soon unsaved loved ones.

**The Wonders of Keukenhof Gardens –
Clothed by the best!**

Did you know that Nature is a top-notch designer? In fact, I can say God is the Master Designer. He matches colors in perfect hues, nothing is ever out of place.

During our very first Women's Conference at the Ambassadors Church in Kuala Lumpur, Malaysia, Pastor Lisa and I had the privilege of having our colors done by Hannelie, whom you read about in this book. I was accustomed to wearing whatever I liked until I was matched with the most suitable color pallet for me.

Twice in my life, I've had the distinct pleasure of visiting Keukenhof Gardens in Holland. Keukenhof is a park where more than 7 million flower bulbs are planted every year. Gardens and four pavilions show a fantastic collection of tulips, hyacinths, daffodils, orchids, roses, carnations, irises, lilies, and many other flowers.

Today's shape and appearance of the park dates to the distant 1857 and was created by the famous architect, Jan David Zocher. The park consists of many gardens and four pavilions where the whole history and tradition of Tulip cultivation in the Netherlands is displayed.

In 2016, their season's opening corresponded with a visit from my good friend, Edwina, whom I lovingly refer to as Lady E., a Lady in every sense of the word and one of the most dedicated hostesses I've had the pleasure of knowing. She and her husband, Pastor John, are the new leaders of our church in Malaysia.

We visited that outrageously beautiful garden along with many other tulip and flower admirers. Our gaze rested upon row after row of perfected magnificent colors, as we beheld their beauty and inhaled the tantalizing fragrance of each unique flower. The Lord says in Matthew 6:28-30 NIV, *"And why do you worry about clothes? See how the flowers of the field grow. They do not labor or spin. Yet I tell you that not even Solomon in all his splendor was dressed like one of these.*

If that is how God clothes the grass of the field, which is here today and tomorrow is thrown into the fire, will he not much more clothe you — you of little faith?"

Faith comes from the hearing of God's Word. I was able to savor it and believe that God would provide for my needs just as he does for the birds of the air and clothe me like the flowers of the field. Just as the greenhouses develop the beautiful flowers in Keukenhof's garden, I believe our Father has a heavenly storehouse where He provides for us. The greenhouse must have favorable conditions to grow beautiful plants and so we must also be in favorable conditions to grow under the Holy Spirit's supervision.

When I first heard teaching on this Scripture, I was a struggling college student, in dire need of financial assistance. I had just studied about the scientist Maslow and his hierarchy of needs where he states a human's basic needs are self-actualization, esteem, love, belonging, safety, and physiological needs. I felt I needed much more! What was missing out of that pyramid was Christ!

We must abide in His Word and beware of the one who comes to sow tares while we're sleeping. The Bible says in Matthew 13:25 NIV -- *"But that night as the workers slept, his enemy came and planted weeds among the wheat, then slipped away."* Weeds choke the wheat just as problems choke the Word which has been planted in our hearts. As soon as we hear the Word and gain faith, persecution comes to negate that faith! We must remain persistent and abide in Christ.

In the very first garden, there was no pollution, only beauty and purity and the man and the woman. Satan came to the woman to sow doubt in the Garden of Eden. If you don't keep watch, he will also come to your magnificently manicured garden and sow doubt and destruction.

This year (2021), I was away from my home for two and a half months, working in another state. My husband, too, had traveled to France and The Netherlands. When we were away, a lone wild pig came to our property and destroyed our lawn. In addition, our gardener did not take proper care of our real estate and weeds took over. This left an incredible mess for my husband and me to sort out.

At Keukenhof, they must be careful to remove the weeds and disease-forming fungus to create the beauty that we all behold when we visit that garden. And so, the Master Designer must do the same for us!

The wonders of Keukenhof are never ending. Rows and glorious rows of exquisitely hand-crafted flowers painted by the Master Designer. Rhonda with Lady Edwina to the right.

Eiffel Tower

The beauty of being an expat is having friends all over the world and getting a chance to visit them!

In June of 2016, we traveled to France to celebrate the High School graduation of the daughter of my friend, Dana. She lives in a spacious apartment facing the Seine River and the Eiffel Tower is so close, it feels as if you can reach out to touch it. At dawn I would sit out on her balcony and behold the beauty of it all. The Seine River representing the Holy Spirit refreshing my thirsty soul.

The Seine River is known for its romantic sightseeing boats, called "bateaux mouches," that drift up and down the river in Paris. Dams and locks normally keep the water level consistent, particularly in the Paris region, where the Seine's traffic is especially heavy, in part because of tourist and other recreational vessels.

Throughout the Word of God, water is a symbol, a type of the Spirit of God, and is often used as an analogy to represent Holy Spirit, that is, the divine nature and power of God. Jesus said to the sinful woman at the well in John 4:14 NIV -- *"But those who drink the water I give will never be thirsty again. It becomes a fresh, bubbling spring within them, giving them eternal life."*

The Seine River represented the Holy Spirit to me, and the Eiffel Tower reminded me of how our God is a strong tower.

The impressionable scene on my friend's balcony made me understand the grandiose nature of our God even the more. How we can feel safe in His everlasting arms, and how we are renewed daily by the living Word and cleansed by the Holy Spirit living within us, as a deposit and promise of our Eternal Life which awaits us at the end of this life's earthly journey! Blessed Assurance!

The Ascent – Hiking in the Mountains

I arrived in the French mountains a mere 7 days ago, but the progress I have made in hiking up and down the mountainous terrain has been nothing short of a miracle! I have gone from barely being able to make the ascent, to hiking 8 to 11 km. per day! What a marvelous feat!

The Bible says when the Israelites ascended the mountain toward Jerusalem they sang. One thing I have learned about our Christian walk is, that one day we are on the mountain top and the next, in the valley! Life circumstances have put our emotions all over the place, yet God admonishes us to speak to the mountain and it shall be moved out of its place.

The Songs of Ascent are a special group of psalms comprising Psalms 120 -134. They are also called Pilgrim Songs. Four of these songs are attributed to King

David (122, 124, 131, 133) and one to Solomon (127), while the remaining ten are anonymous.

The city of Jerusalem is situated on a high hill. Jews traveling to Jerusalem for one of the three main annual Jewish festivals traditionally sang these songs on the "ascent" or the uphill road to the city. According to some traditions, the Jewish priests also sang some of these Songs of Ascent as they walked up the steps to the Temple in Jerusalem.

Each of the psalms in this collection begins with the title "A Song of Ascents." While perhaps they were not originally composed for this purpose, these psalms were later grouped together for use in traveling toward Jerusalem for the yearly Jewish festivals.

The theme of each Song of Ascent offers much encouragement for those who seek to worship God today:

Psalm 120: God's presence during distress
Psalm 121: Joyful praise to the Lord
Psalm 122: Prayer for Jerusalem
Psalm 123: Patience for God's mercy
Psalm 124: Help comes from the Lord
Psalm 125: Prayer for God's blessing upon His people
Psalm 126: The Lord has done great things
Psalm 127: God's blessing on man's efforts
Psalm 128: Joy for those who follow God's ways
Psalm 129: A cry for help to the Lord
Psalm 130: A prayer of repentance
Psalm 131: Surrender as a child to the Lord
Psalm 132: God's sovereign plan for His people
Psalm 133: Praise of brotherly fellowship and unity
Psalm 134 : Praise to God in His temple

The Songs of Ascent continue to find a place among the many hymns and songs of worship of Jews and Christians today. They serve as powerful examples of how we can express our worship and love for God through the power of song.

Please write your prayer here and include a scripture reference for each request.

_____

_____

Making mountains into plains:

Zerubbabel said, "Nothing, not even a mighty mountain, will stand in Zerubbabel's way; it will become a level plain before him! And when Zerubbabel sets the final stone of the Temple in place, the people will shout: 'May God bless it! May God bless it!'" (Zechariah 4:7 NIV).

What are you saying? What are you seeing, a mountain or a plain? What comes out of your mouth will be an important weapon for your success in overcoming what stands in your way!

One thing I learned from hiking in the French mountains is that you must have determination and stamina. These 2 ingredients are necessary for you to complete your climb. Giving up was not an option as I was with my petite, yet tenacious trainer who had been in the military. Giving up had never been an option. Zerrubabel, too, was not daunted by the mountain before him. He spoke to it, and it was made level as a plain.

Today you might be facing a mountain of finances, disappointment, sickness, marital or children's issues. No matter the problem, the same formular may be applied. I dare you to take up Zerubbabel's stance by saying, "Who are you before _____?" (Place your name in the blank to make your ground level)!

Mountain:
PPS - Plain Prayer Solution/Scripture for the mountain to become a level plain.

Scripture

The Resting Place

There are times when the Lord gives you a respite and, dear Sisters, I recommend you take it. With Elijah, during the famine, the Lord fed him, "Then the word of the Lord came to Elijah: *'Leave here, turn eastward, and hide in the Kerith Ravine, east of the Jordan. You will drink from the brook, and I have directed the ravens to supply you with food there.'*" (1 Kings 17:2-4 NIV).

The Lord fed Elijah miraculously by ravens, which are scavengers.

The Lord bade me take rest and do nothing for seven days. If you know me this was an incredibly difficult task. I was staying with my friend and her family in the French Alps, in a small village that borders Geneva where you can see the French Alps and Mont Blanc towering majestically in the backdrop. Yet I found myself trying to be useful by helping to prepare meals and help clean. My friend's children were so well trained that it was truly hard to help. By day 4, I relented to rest and began writing again.

Listening and obeying the voice of the Lord is paramount in our Faith Walk. He, alone, knows our future, not the fortune-teller reading our palm who uses divination, or the person who dabbles in spiritism and uses a spirit-guide. None are omnipresent like our Lord, Jehovah Shammah. The Lord has admonished that we do not seek after these to know our future, He alone knows.

In 2000, I was on vacation in my native Alabama. The Spirit of the Lord beckoned me to "The Secret Place". At that time, we had recently purchased and refurbished a small two-bedroom property around 18 miles from my mom's place. While Clement, my husband, entertained the twins, I requested a room in my friend Zaida's basement where I could pray and listen to God.

At that time, I had no trial in my life but the Almighty, All-seeing God knew what was up ahead. I heard the Lord impress in my spirit, "Go, daughter, to the secret place and let me equip you for this upcoming battle. I want you to be reassured that my plans for you are good plans, plans not to harm you, plans to give you hope and a future." This voice or impression was spoken to my heart through a Rhema Word which I later discovered in Jeremiah 29:11 NIV.

I had no foreboding, no apprehension and certainly no expectation other than that God wanted good for my life. I left the secret place and returned to my mom's when Clement left the country. Trying to decide whether to continue my fast, I decided to take my mom out to eat. The next day, early in the morning, I received a call that had the potential to rock my world, everything I had built my faith on thus far risked shattering. I was emotionally, spiritually, and physically distraught. With my husband thousands of miles away, I sought wise counsel from my pastors as well as my mom. Then I remembered the word the Lord had given me while in The Secret Place. "Daughter, be still and know that I am God. For I know the plans I have for you, declares the Lord, plans to prosper you and not to harm you, plans to give you hope and a future."

These mere words from Abba brought hope and reassurance. My tipped world sought to steady back in its place. Elijah had received nourishment from ravens, and later, weary from his journey, an angel fed him. He had been strengthened and enabled to continue his journey, that Secret Place experience had the same effect on me! Had I not hearkened to the voice of the Lord and spent that time in prayer, my outcome might have been different!

You may also employ this Scripture Meal for the circumstances that you are currently facing. If your world has been rocked like mine, you will have strength for the journey.

"Be still before the Lord
  and wait patiently for him..."
(Psalm 37:7a NIV).

"For I know the plans I have for you," declares the Lord, *"plans to prosper you and not to harm you, plans to give you hope and a future."* (Jeremiah 29: 11 NIV)

The Liberating Dance of Africa

At last the night is over.
The dawn has turned to day.
Reminiscing on my days in Paris,
how the sun rose like a big orange flame illuminating the one in my heart.
Does the sun of Europe look the same as the one of Africa?
The one that rises in sorrow and deep wails of pitiful cries.

The sound at first is inaudible but escalates to such a terrifying pitch -
Such a piercing, pitiful sound,
yet amid the suffering,
no one is there with comforting arms.
No-one notices where the stifled now muffled moans are coming from.

And then she is seen, with outstretched arms towards the Heavens.
She prays for her lost soul.
She prays for her African sisters of days past and present who have sung those same sorrowful tunes.
Whose sufferings brought desolation and destruction in their lives.
Alas, she rises!
At first, she appears to stumble but then she balances herself.

She dances now to the rhythm of her sad, sorrowful sobs.
The 'tam tam' of that Dark Continent beat and accompanies her liberating dance.
There is no need for rehearsal, Africa is familiar with this tune,
She has played it countless times before.

Then something unexpectedly happens.
Her sorrow turns into joy.
The sun that once scorched her parched dry lands now brings life.
The rays of the 'Son' are so bright that they pierce into her darkness, illuminating every obscure corner of her life.
Her soul is first returned,
then her spirit,
and lastly her body.
She will live.
For she has willed herself to do so.
(For she who the SON sets free is FREE INDEED John 8:36 Paraphrased).

Rhonda Dikoko, February 2005

This poem is the culmination of nearly 365 days being out of the will of God and perceiving I was absent from His Presence. What a wretched soul I was to feel divorced from God! I was an enemy of the Most High and I lived in fear. I finally clearly understood this verse of scripture:

Hebrews 6:4-6 which says, *"4For it is impossible to bring back to repentance those who were once enlightened – those who have experienced the good things of heaven and shared in the Holy Spirit, 5 who have tasted the goodness of the word of God and the power of the age to come – 6 and who then turn away from God. It is impossible to bring such people back to repentance; by rejecting the Son of God, they themselves are nailing him to the cross once again and holding him up to public shame."*

You see it is our conscience and shame that fool us into believing we are beyond Redemption. It is the voice in our head that reasons with us about our sins and causes us to bear our own cross unnecessarily.

It is impossible for someone who has been enlightened in the Word and to turn their back if they hearken to the Holy Spirit. The problem with folk is that they hear the voice of the Holy Spirit and continue in that sin allowing themselves to become callous and immune to hearing the voice of God. Their conscience becomes seared, sin attaches itself with its deadly tentacles. The only way out is sincere repentance, confession and returning wholeheartedly to God never to return to your filth again! The problem with sin is it is pleasurable to the sinful nature. The flesh enjoys partaking of the forbidden fruit.

However, the Word of God says in 1 John 3:9-10, *"⁹ No one who is born of God will continue to sin, because God's seed remains in them; they cannot go on sinning, because they have been born of God. ¹⁰ This is how we know who the children of God are and who the children of the devil are: Anyone who does not do what is right is not God's child, nor is anyone who does not love their brother and sister."*

This passage is very clear on our stance as Believers. We are from the 'Grace Generation,' but this does not give us the right to continuously sin. There is a new covenant that the Lord has established with his people based on knowing who he is. Having that intimate relationship with Abba that we spoke of earlier.

This is the covenant I will establish with the people of Israel
   after that time, declares the Lord.
I will put my laws in their minds
   and write them on their hearts.
I will be their God,
   and they will be my people.
¹¹ No longer will they teach their neighbor,
   or say to one another, 'Know the Lord,'
because they will all know me,
   from the least of them to the greatest.
¹² For I will forgive their wickedness
   and will remember their sins no more.
¹³ By calling this covenant "new," he has made the first one obsolete; and what is obsolete and outdated will soon disappear (Hebrews 8: 10-13 NIV).

As for me, I felt the Lord on every turn beckoning me to return. I felt nauseated from my own sin and not worthy of saving.

Let's be clear, although I was intentional about choosing my OWN way and turning from God, I was fully aware of where I had erred and had a desire to return to God with all of my heart. During that year of wandering knowing full well the correct path to take, I lived in fear every time I chose NOT to take it. I lived in a perpetual cycle in the Valley of decision.

"Thousands upon thousands are waiting in the valley of decision. There the day of the LORD will soon arrive." (Joel 3:14).

That year I experienced what it was like to be living for my own self, I also experienced the redeeming power of Almighty God, the Messiah, Our Lord and Savior. Praise God!

John 8:36 declares, *"So if the Son sets you free, you will be free indeed."*

Like Job, I reasoned with the Lord. It was a conversation that went something like this.

"Abba, this thing, this sin that so easily besets me, is keeping me from worshiping you properly. I cry all day and all night, yet I have no relief!"

But you said in your Word, *"No temptation has overtaken you, but such as is common to man; and God is faithful, He will not allow you to be tempted beyond what you are able, but with the temptation will provide the way of escape also, so that you will be able to endure it."* (1 Corinthians 10.13 NASB).

Father continues speaking through his Word:

"There is a pathway that seems right to a man, but in the end it's a road to death." (Proverbs 14:12 ISV).

"But for you who fear my name, the Sun of righteousness will rise with healing in his wings. And you will go free, leaping with joy like calves let out to pasture." (Malachi 4:2 NLT).

My response to the voice of the Lord:

"Set me free Lord from every sin that entangles me! Rise, oh Son of Righteousness, with healing in your wings! You are my Righteousness, my Jehovah Tsidkenu. I am in right standing with God not because of anything I do, but because of all that you have done! For you have said in your Sacred Word in Romans 3:21-26, "Christ took our punishment for sin. People are made right with God when they believe that Jesus sacrificed his life, shedding his blood. This sacrifice shows that God was being fair when he held back and did not punish those who sinned in times past, for he was looking ahead and including them in what he would do in this present time. God did this to demonstrate his righteousness, for he himself is fair and just, and he makes sinners right in his sight when they believe in Jesus.*

The Lord said:

Daughter, *"God saved you by his grace when you believed. And you can't take credit for this; it is a gift from God."* (Ephesians 2: 8 NLT). Amen. Selah.

Prayer:

Lord, I take this free gift you have so graciously extended to me. In fact, I realize that you were there with me all along. For your Word declares that nothing can separate me from the Love of God.

³¹"What shall we say about such wonderful things as these? If God is for us, who can ever be against us? ³² Since he did not spare even his own Son but gave him up for us all, won't he also give us everything else? ³³ Who dares accuse us whom God has chosen for his own? No one—for God himself has given us right standing with himself. ³⁴ Who then will condemn us? No one—for Christ Jesus died for us and was raised to life for us, and he is sitting in the place of honor at God's right hand, pleading for us. ³⁵ Can anything ever separate us from Christ's love? Does it mean he no longer loves us if we have trouble or calamity, or are persecuted, or hungry, or destitute, or in danger, or threatened with death? ³⁶(As the Scriptures say, "For your sake we are killed every day; we are being slaughtered like sheep.") ³⁷ No, despite all these things, overwhelming victory is ours through Christ, who loved us. ³⁸And I am convinced that nothing can ever separate us from God's love. Neither death nor life, neither angels nor demons, neither our fears for today nor our worries about tomorrow—not even the powers of hell can separate us from God's love. ³⁹ No power in the sky above or in the earth below— indeed, nothing in all creation will ever be able to separate us from the love of God that is revealed in Christ Jesus our Lord." (Romans 8:31-39).

A Call to Salvation

If you are a child of the King today, you have been made righteous in Christ Jesus – Jehovah Tsidkenu – God, our Righteousness. He takes His righteousness and puts it upon us (Zechariah 3:3-6 NIV). Then he covers you with a thick white impenetrable garment similar to how he caps the majestic Mont Blanc in all of its glory.

Jehovah Tsidkenu changes your filthy garment of sin into sparkling radiant raiment of pure white. Only He can do this. Eternity speaks, today, if you hear His voice, do not harden your heart.

If you have yet to surrender your life to Jesus, I plead with you to hand over the reins of your life to Him today. Repeat this prayer below:

Dear Lord Jesus, I admit that I am a sinner saved by your grace alone.

Forgive me for my sins. I believe you died for me and rose again on the 3rd day. Cleanse me today, oh Lord, and I shall be clean. Thank you for this invitation of new life. Fill me Lord with your peace, presence, and power. Help me from this day forward to build my life in you. Give me a home in your Kingdom, in Jesus' Name I have prayed. Amen.

Abiding in Christ

In John 15, there is the story of the vinedresser who cuts off every branch which does not bear fruit.

When you enter into a covenant relationship with the Lord you begin to have Kingdom privileges not previously accessible to you. You devour His Word and begin to have your mind transformed and renewed. You begin to conform your life to His commandments. The main one is that if we abide in Him, and His words abide in us, we will ask what we will, and we'll receive it.

Read John 15 and learn how to be a proper disciple of Christ. Find a Church on-line or in person that can help you on your journey to knowing Christ better. Get baptized in water and seek the Baptism of the Holy Spirit.

Would you write to me and tell me about your decision? I would be delighted to pray for you!

Paul's benediction in Galatians 8:14-18 NIV:

14 "May I never boast except in the cross of our Lord Jesus Christ, through which the world has been crucified to me, and I to the world. 15 Neither circumcision nor uncircumcision means anything; what counts is the new creation. 16 Peace and mercy to all who follow this rule—to the Israel of God. 17 From now on, let no one cause me trouble, for I bear on my body the marks of Jesus. 18 The grace of our Lord Jesus Christ be with your spirit, brothers, and sisters." Amen.

Epilogue – By Fabien Zinga

Go ye therefore, and teach all nations, baptizing them in the name of the Father, and of the Son, and of the Holy Ghost:
Teaching them to observe all things whatsoever I have commanded you: and, lo, I am with you always, even unto the end of the world. Amen.
                                             Matthew 28: 19-20 (KJV, emphasis added)

And the things that *thou hast heard of me* among many witnesses, the same *commit thou to faithful men*, who shall be able *to teach others also*.
                                             2 Timothy 2:2 (KJV, emphasis added)

Remember *your leaders*, those who *spoke to you the word of God*. Consider the outcome of their way of life and *imitate their faith*.
                                             Hebrews 13:7 (ESV, emphasis added)

One generation shall commend your works to another and shall declare your mighty acts.
                                             Psalms 145: 4 (ESV, emphasis added)

We are now at the end of this inspirational book: *The Sacred Words of a Sage Femme*. Or are we? I believe this is only the beginning, better yet, the continuation of the ministry of the Holy Spirit in Rhonda Wilson Dikoko into the lives of her spiritual children across the globe. If you are blessed like I am to have known and learned from Mama Rhonda, it is now your responsibility to mentor and become a "sage femme" to someone else. The same way Mama Rhonda has helped birth your dreams and launch you into your destiny and purpose, you too must help others discover their purpose and achieve their God-given dreams.

At the tender age of twelve years old, I first met Rhonda Wilson Dikoko back in 1990 at a gospel meeting she organized at a local hotel in Pointe-Noire, the Republic of the Congo, my original home. I had just been born again at a Full Gospel Business Men's Fellowship International meeting led by both my uncles, Thomas Kinouani and Dr. Pastor Jérémie Kinouani, not long before. I had never heard a person preach the gospel the way she did.
Thirty-two years later, I still remember what she talked about that night; it literally changed my life.

Mama Rhonda shared with me the keys to the kingdom of God. She planted seeds in my heart that would later blossom into total harvests, starting me on a path to develop a personal relationship with Jesus that would literally blow my mind, taking me on a journey above and beyond my wildest dreams, anything I could have ever thought or imagined. I still remember spending several mornings in her house listening to the wisdom of the word of God and learning African American urban gospel songs. I remember it as if it were yesterday.

Jesus, who is our ultimate example, said, "Go," "Teach," and "[Teach] them to observe all things whatsoever I have commanded you." The same teaching, I have received from Mama Rhonda, who has traveled worldwide, in almost every continent, including Africa, where she found me, I will teach others wherever I go. The same Jesus she preached to me; I will preach to people I meet everywhere I go. I will also preach to others that same gospel that she has preached to me which has worked for me, delivered me, healed me, set me free, and prospered and blessed me.

That which I have received from Mama Rhonda, I will commit to teach others who shall in turn be able to teach and reach even more people. I will never be able to pay back Mama Rhonda for being so in tune with the Holy Spirit and giving so much of herself to people she did not even know, but this one thing I can do is teach the same kingdom principles to at least someone else. I can imitate her faith and expect God to produce the same outcome in the lives of those who will take time to hear 'Thus Saith the Lord!" It is now up to me and you to commend the works of the Lord to the next generation, to declare His mighty acts!

Don't just be inspired by the beautiful stories of redemption, grace, miracles, and wonders found on the pages of this book, but be moved to action.

Act to be a conduit of the Holy Spirit, the same way God has used Mama Rhonda to impact your life, impact the lives of the people of your generation. Pass it forward by mentoring, praying, and standing in the gap for someone else in need within the sphere of your influence. May we all aspire to be more like Mama Rhonda and love the Lord with all of our hearts and people without abandon. The only Jesus, many in the world, will see is the manifestation of Jesus and His love in us.

Like Mama Rhonda, let's be a living epistle, a living testimony to God's love, grace, and power to a hurting and sinful world. Don't wait, be a "sage femme" to someone else. Let the Word which is in you, overflow out of your being impacting the lives of those you come in contact with everywhere you go, redeeming the time, because the days are evil.

Bob Fabien Zinga with his wife Demetria Zinga
Spiritual Son of Rhonda Wilson Dikoko
Care Pastor, Redemption Church, San Jose, CA, USA

Postlude

I sincerely hope these *Re-stories* presented in this book have put a stirring deep down in your spirit and soul. If a story has resonated in your innermost being moving you to action, then my purpose would have been accomplished.

Go forward with the message of the gospel and with the determination to make disciples everywhere you go! Stir up your God-given gifts. The Bible says in 2 Timothy 1:6-7, *'Therefore, I remind you, to stir up the gift of God which is in you through the laying on of my hands. For God has not given us a spirit of fear, but of power and of love and of a sound mind."* Be a *Sage Femme* or endeavor to mentor someone else!

The third *Sage Femme* I mentioned in my Acknowledgements, is Sister Sarah Banks. I had the honor of travelling with her for years serving as her personal interpreter during crusades in Africa and Europe. She was by far one of the most influential Spiritual *Sage Femmes* in my life. Just this month, she was elevated to eternity. And although I love and miss her so deeply, losing her has given me a greater appreciation of the magnificent reunion one day we will experience in Glory!

My prayer is that if you and I don't meet on earth here below, we will meet in our heavenly abode.

In His Service.

Evangelist Rhonda,
Sage Femme

Lady Wisdom Calls Out (Proverbs 8, The Message)

1-11 Do you hear Lady Wisdom calling?
   Can you hear Madame Insight raising her voice?
She's taken her stand at First and Main,
   at the busiest intersection.
Right in the city square
   where the traffic is thickest, she shouts,
"You—I'm talking to all of you,
   everyone out here on the streets!
Listen, you idiots—learn good sense!
   You blockheads—shape up!
Don't miss a word of this—I'm telling you how to live well,
   I'm telling you how to live at your best.
My mouth chews and savors and relishes truth—
   I can't stand the taste of evil!
You'll only hear true and right words from my mouth;
   not one syllable will be twisted or skewed.
You'll recognize this as true—you with open minds;
   truth-ready minds will see it at once.
Prefer my life-disciplines over chasing after money,
   and God-knowledge over a lucrative career.
For Wisdom is better than all the trappings of wealth;
   nothing you could wish for holds a candle to her.
12-21 "I am Lady Wisdom, and I live next to Sanity;
   Knowledge and Discretion live just down the street.
The Fear-of-GOD means hating Evil,
   whose ways I hate with a passion—
   pride and arrogance and crooked talk.
Good counsel and common sense are my characteristics;
   I am both Insight and the Virtue to live it out.
With my help, leaders rule,
   and lawmakers legislate fairly;
With my help, governors govern,
   along with all in legitimate authority.
I love those who love me;
   those who look for me find me.
Wealth and Glory accompany me—
   also substantial Honor and a Good Name.
My benefits are worth more than a big salary, even a very big salary;
   the returns on me exceed any imaginable bonus.
You can find me on Righteous Road—that's where I walk—
   at the intersection of Justice Avenue,
Handing out life to those who love me,
   filling their arms with life—armloads of life!

22-31 "GOD sovereignly made me—the first, the basic—
 before he did anything else.
I was brought into being a long time ago,
 well before Earth got its start.
I arrived on the scene before Ocean,
 yes, even before Springs and Rivers and Lakes.
Before Mountains were sculpted and Hills took shape,
 I was already there, newborn;
Long before GOD stretched out Earth's Horizons,
 and tended to the minute details of Soil and Weather,
And set Sky firmly in place,
 I was there.
When he mapped and gave borders to wild Ocean,
 built the vast vault of Heaven,
 and installed the fountains that fed Ocean,
When he drew a boundary for Sea,
 posted a sign that said NO TRESPASSING,
And then staked out Earth's Foundations,
 I was right there with him, making sure everything fit.
Day after day I was there, with my joyful applause,
 always enjoying his company,
Delighted with the world of things and creatures,
 happily celebrating the human family.
32-36 "So, my dear friends, listen carefully;
 those who embrace these my ways are most blessed.
Mark a life of discipline and live wisely;
 don't squander your precious life.
Blessed the man, blessed the woman, who listens to me,
 awake and ready for me each morning,
 alert and responsive as I start my day's work.
When you find me, you find life, real life,
 to say nothing of GOD's good pleasure.
But if you wrong me, you damage your very soul;
 when you reject me, you're flirting with death."

References

www.gotquestionabibibla.com

www.ccbirthcenter.com

www./christainitybible/bible.com

Other Books and Products by Rhonda Wilson-Dikoko

Release the Dove Book
Release the Dove Workbook
Release the Dove Devotional
Release the Dove T-Shirt
Release the Dove bag

www.amazon.com

Rhonda Dikoko – YouTube – Release the Dove Ministry Series
Rhonda Dikoko Release the Dove – Facebook Page
wilsondikoko@outlook.com

www.ingramcontent.com/pod-product-compliance
Lightning Source LLC
Chambersburg PA
CBHW040317240426
43665CB00030B/2970